THE INTERNATIONAL
PSYCHO - ANALYTICAL
LIBRARY

THE INTERNATIONAL PSYCHO-ANALYTICAL LIBRARY

EDITED BY ERNEST JONES, M.D.

GROUP PSYCHOLOGY AND THE ANALYSIS OF THE EGO

SIGMUND FREUD, MD., LL.D.

AUTHORIZED TRANSLATION BY

JAMES STRACHEY

LIVERIGHT PUBLISHING CORPORATION

NEW YORK

1951

First published 1922
Sixth impression 1951

Printed in Great Britain by
Lowe and Brydone Printers Limited, London, N.W.10

TRANSLATOR'S NOTE

A comparison of the following pages with the German original (*Massenpsychologie und Ich-Analyse*, Internationaler Psychoanalytischer Verlag, Vienna, 1921) will show that certain passages have been transferred in the English version from the text to the footnotes. This alteration has been carried out at the author's express desire.

All technical terms have been translated in accordance with the Glossary to be published as a supplement to the *International Journal of Psycho-Analysis*.

J. S.

CONTENTS

GROUP PSYCHOLOGY AND
THE ANALYSIS OF THE EGO

I
INTRODUCTION

The contrast between Individual Psychology and Social or Group[1] Psychology, which at a first glance may seem to be full of significance, loses a great deal of its sharpness when it is examined more closely. It is true that Individual Psychology is concerned with the individual man and explores the paths by which he seeks to find satisfaction for his instincts; but only rarely and under certain exceptional conditions is Individual Psychology in a position to disregard the relations of this individual to others. In the individual's mental life someone else is invariably involved, as a

[1] ['Group' is used throughout this translation as equivalent to the rather more comprehensive German '*Masse*'. The author uses this latter word to render both McDougall's 'group', and also Le Bon's '*foule*', which would more naturally be translated 'crowd' in English. For the sake of uniformity, however, 'group' has been preferred in this case as well, and has been substituted for 'crowd' even in the extracts from the English translation of Le Bon.—*Translator.*]

model, as an object, as a helper, as an opponent, and so from the very first Individual Psychology is at the same time Social Psychology as well—in this extended but entirely justifiable sense of the words.

The relations of an individual to his parents and to his brothers and sisters, to the object of his love, and to his physician—in fact all the relations which have hitherto been the chief subject of psycho-analytic research—may claim to be considered as social phenomena; and in this respect they may be contrasted with certain other processes, described by us as 'narcissistic', in which the satisfaction of the instincts is partially or totally withdrawn from the influence of other people. The contrast between social and narcissistic—Bleuler would perhaps call them 'autistic'—mental acts therefore falls wholly within the domain of Individual Psychology, and is not well calculated to differentiate it from a Social or Group Psychology.

The individual in the relations which have already been mentioned—to his parents and to his brothers and sisters, to the person he is in love with, to his friend, and to his physician—comes under the influence of only a single person, or of a very small number of persons, each one of whom has become enormously important to him. Now in speaking of Social or Group Psychology it has become usual to leave these relations on one side and to isolate as the subject of inquiry the influencing of an individual by a large number of people simultaneously, people with whom he is connected by something, though otherwise they may in many respects be strangers to him. Group Psychology is therefore concerned with the individual man as a member of a race, of a nation, of a caste, of a profession, of an institution, or as a component part of a crowd of people who have been organised into a group at some particular time for some definite purpose. When once natural continuity has been severed in this way, it is easy to regard the phenomena that appear under these special conditions as being expressions of a special instinct that is not further reducible, the social instinct ('herd instinct', 'group mind'), which does not come to light in any other situations. But we may perhaps venture to object that it seems difficult to attribute to the factor of number a significance so great as to make it capable by itself of arousing in our mental life a new instinct that is otherwise not brought into play. Our expectation is therefore directed towards two other possibilities: that the social instinct may not be a primitive one and insusceptible of dissection, and that it may be possible to discover the beginnings of its development in a narrower circle, such as that of the family.

Although Group Psychology is only in its infancy, it embraces an immense number of separate issues and offers to investigators countless problems which have hitherto not even been properly distinguished from one another. The mere classification of the different forms of group formation and the description of the mental phenomena produced by them require a great expenditure of observation and exposition, and have already given rise to a copious literature. Anyone who compares the narrow dimensions of this little book with the extent of Group Psychology will at once be able to guess that only a few points chosen from the whole material are to be dealt with here. And they will in fact only be a few questions with which the depth-psychology of psycho-analysis is specially concerned.

II

LE BON'S DESCRIPTION OF THE GROUP MIND

Instead of starting from a definition, it seems more useful to begin with some indication of the range of the phenomena under review, and to select from among them a few specially striking and characteristic facts to which our inquiry can be attached. We can achieve both of these aims by means of quotation from Le Bon's deservedly famous work *Psychologie des foules*.[1]

Let us make the matter clear once again. If a Psychology, concerned with exploring the predispositions, the instincts, the motives and the aims of an individual man down to his actions and his relations with those who are nearest to him, had completely achieved its task, and had cleared up the whole of these matters with their inter-connections, it would then suddenly find itself confronted by a new task which would lie before it unachieved. It would be

[1] *The Crowd: a Study of the Popular Mind*. Fisher Unwin, 12th. Impression, 1920.

obliged to explain the surprising fact that under a certain condition this individual whom it had come to understand thought, felt, and acted in quite a different way from what would have been expected. And this condition is his insertion into a collection of people which has acquired the characteristic of a 'psychological group'. What, then, is a 'group'? How does it acquire the capacity for exercising such a decisive infl   over the mental life of the individual? And ...   he nature of the mental change which it force   ,on the individual?

It is the task of a theoretical Group Psychology to answer these three questions. The best way of approaching them is evidently to start with the third. Observation of the changes in the individual's reactions is what provides Group Psychology with its material; for every attempt at an explanation must be preceded by a description of the thing that is to be explained.

I will now let Le Bon speak for himself. He says: 'The most striking peculiarity presented by a psychological group[1] is the following. Whoever be the individuals that compose it, however like or unlike be their mode of life, their occupations, their character, or their intelligence, the fact that they have been transformed into a group puts them in possession of a sort of collective mind which makes

[1] [See footnote page i.]

them feel, think, and act in a manner quite different
from that in which each individual of them would
feel, think, and act were he in a state of isolation.
There are certain ideas and feelings which do not
come into being, or do not transform themselves into
acts except in the case of individuals forming a group.
The psychological group is a provisional being formed
of heterogeneous elements, which for a moment are
combined, exactly as the cells which constitute a
living body form by their reunion a new being which
displays characteristics very different from those
possessed by each of the cells singly.' (p. 29.)[1]

We shall take the liberty of interrupting Le
Bon's exposition with glosses of our own, and shall
accordingly insert an observation at this point. If
the individuals in the group are combined into a
unity, there must surely be something to unite them,
and this bond might be precisely the thing that is
characteristic of a group. But Le Bon does not answer
this question; he goes on to consider the alteration
which the individual undergoes when in a group and
describes it in terms which harmonize well with the
fundamental postulates of our own depth-psychology.

'It is easy to prove how much the individual
forming part of a group differs from the isolated
individual, but it is less easy to discover the causes
of this difference.

[1] [References are to the English translation.—*Translator.*]

'To obtain at any rate a glimpse of them it is necessary in the first place to call to mind the truth established by modern psychology, that unconscious phenomena play an altogether preponderating part not only in organic life, but also in the operations of the intelligence. The conscious life of the mind is of small importance in comparison with its unconscious life. The most subtle analyst, the most acute observer, is scarcely successful in discovering more than a very small number of the conscious[1] motives that determine his conduct. Our conscious acts are the outcome of an unconscious substratum created in the mind in the main by hereditary influences. This substratum consists of the innumerable common characteristics handed down from generation to generation, which constitute the genius of a race. Behind the avowed causes of our acts there undoubtedly lie secret causes that we do not avow, but behind these secret causes there are many others more secret still, of which we ourselves are ignorant.[2] The greater part of our daily actions are the result of hidden motives which escape our observation.' (p. 30.)

[1] [The German translation of Le Bon, quoted by the author, reads '*bewusster*'; the English translation has 'unconscious'; and the original French text '*inconscients*'.—*Translator*.]

[2] [The English translation reads 'which we ourselves ignore'— a misunderstanding of the French word '*ignorées*'.—*Translator*.]

Le Bon thinks that the particular acquirements of individuals become obliterated in a group, and that in this way their distinctiveness vanishes. The racial unconscious emerges; what is heterogeneous is submerged in what is homogeneous. We may say that the mental superstructure, the development of which in individuals shows such dissimilarities, is removed, and that the unconscious foundations, which are similar in everyone, stand exposed to view.

In this way individuals in a group would come to show an average character. But Le Bon believes that they also display new characteristics which they have not previously possessed, and he seeks the reason for this in three different factors.

'The first is that the individual forming part of a group acquires, solely from numerical considerations, a sentiment of invincible power which allows him to yield to instincts which, had he been alone, he would perforce have kept under restraint. He will be the less disposed to check himself from the consideration that, a group being anonymous, and in consequence irresponsible, the sentiment of responsibility which always controls individuals disappears entirely.' (p. 33.)

From our point of view we need not attribute so much importance to the appearance of new characteristics. For us it would be enough to say that in a group the individual is brought under conditions which allow him to throw off the repressions

B

of his unconscious instincts. The apparently new characteristics which he then displays are in fact the manifestations of this unconscious, in which all that is evil in the human mind is contained as a predisposition. We can find no difficulty in understanding the disappearance of conscience or of a sense of responsibility in these circumstances. It has long been our contention that 'dread of society [*soziale Angst*]' is the essence of what is called conscience.[1]

'The second cause, which is contagion, also intervenes to determine the manifestation in groups of their special characteristics, and at the same time the trend they are to take. Contagion is a phenomenon of which it is easy to establish the presence, but that it is not easy to explain. It must be classed among those phenomena of a hypnotic order, which we shall shortly study. In a group every sentiment and act is contagious, and contagious to such a

[1] There is some difference between Le Bon's view and ours owing to his concept of the unconscious not quite coinciding with the one adopted by psycho-analysis. Le Bon's unconscious more especially contains the most deeply buried features of the racial mind, which as a matter of fact lies outside the scope of psycho-analysis. We do not fail to recognize, indeed, that the ego's nucleus, which comprises the 'archaic inheritance' of the human mind, is unconscious; but in addition to this we distinguish the 'unconscious repressed', which arose from a portion of that inheritance. This concept of the repressed is not to be found in Le Bon.

degree that an individual readily sacrifices his personal interest to the collective interest. This is an aptitude very contrary to his nature, and of which a man is scarcely capable, except when he makes part of a group.' (p. 33.)

We shall later on base an important conjecture upon this last statement.

'A third cause, and by far the most important, determines in the individuals of a group special characteristics which are quite contrary at times to those presented by the isolated individual. I allude to that suggestibility of which, moreover, the contagion mentioned above is only an effect.

'To understand this phenomenon it is necessary to bear in mind certain recent physiological discoveries. We know to-day that by various processes an individual may be brought into such a condition that, having entirely lost his conscious personality, he obeys all the suggestions of the operator who has deprived him of it, and commits acts in utter contradiction with his character and habits. The most careful investigations seem to prove that an individual immersed for some length of time in a group in action soon finds himself—either in consequence of the magnetic influence given out by the group, or from some other cause of which we are ignorant—in a special state, which much resembles the state of fascination in which the hypnotised individual finds himself in the hands of the hypnotiser. . . . The conscious personality has entirely vanished; will and discernment are lost. All feelings and thoughts are bent in the direction determined by the hypnotiser.

'Such also is approximately the state of the individual forming part of a psychological group. He is no longer conscious of his acts. In his case, as in the case of the hypnotised subject, at the same time that certain faculties are destroyed, others may be brought to a high degree of exaltation. Under the influence of a suggestion, he will undertake the accomplishment of certain acts with irresistible impetuosity. This impetuosity is the more irresistible in the case of groups than in that of the hypnotised subject, from the fact that, the suggestion being the same for all the individuals of the group, it gains in strength by reciprocity.' (p. 34.)

'We see, then, that the disappearance of the conscious personality, the predominance of the unconscious personality, the turning by means of suggestion and contagion of feelings and ideas in an identical direction, the tendency to immediately transform the suggested ideas into acts; these, we see, are the principal characteristics of the individual forming part of a group. He is no longer himself, but has become an automaton who has ceased to be guided by his will.' (p. 35.)

I have quoted this passage so fully in order to make it quite clear that Le Bon explains the condition of an individual in a group as being actually hypnotic, and does not merely make a comparison between the two states. We have no intention of raising any objection at this point, but wish only to emphasize the fact that the two last causes of an individual becoming altered in a group (the contagion and the heightened suggestibility) are evidently not on a par, since the contagion seems actually to be a manifestation of the suggestibility. Moreover the effects of the two factors do not seem to be sharply differentiated in the text of Le Bon's remarks. We may perhaps best interpret his statement if we connect the contagion with the effects of the individual members of the group upon one another, while we point to another source for those manifestations of suggestion in the group which are put on a level with the phenomena of hypnotic influence. But to what source? We cannot avoid being struck with a sense of deficiency when we notice that one of the chief elements of the comparison, namely the person who is to replace the hypnotist in the case of the group, is not mentioned in Le Bon's exposition. But he nevertheless distinguishes between this influence of fascination which remains plunged in obscurity and the contagious effect which the individuals exercise upon one another and by which the original suggestion is strengthened.

Here is yet another important consideration for helping us to understand the individual in a group: 'Moreover, by the mere fact that he forms part of an organised group, a man descends several rungs in the ladder of civilisation. Isolated, he may be a cultivated individual; in a crowd, he is a barbarian— that is, a creature acting by instinct. He possesses the spontaneity, the violence, the ferocity, and also the enthusiasm and heroism of primitive beings.' (p. 36.) He then dwells especially upon the lowering in intellectual ability which an individual experiences when he becomes merged in a group.[1]

Let us now leave the individual, and turn to the group mind, as it has been outlined by Le Bon. It shows not a single feature which a psycho-analyst would find any difficulty in placing or in deriving from its source. Le Bon himself shows us the way by pointing to its similarity with the mental life of primitive people and of children (p. 40).

A group is impulsive, changeable and irritable. It is led almost exclusively by the unconscious.[2] The

[1] Compare Schiller's couplet:
Jeder, sieht man ihn einzeln, ist leidlich klug und verständig;
  Sind sie in corpore, gleich wird euch ein Dummkopf daraus.
[Everyone, seen by himself, is passably shrewd and discerning;
  When they're *in corpore,* then straightway you'll find
                                                    he's an ass.]

[2] 'Unconscious' is used here correctly by Le Bon in the descriptive sense, where it does not only mean the 'repressed'.

impulses which a group obeys may according to circumstances be generous or cruel, heroic or cowardly, but they are always so ⁓⁓⁓ⁱ⁓ⁿs that no personal interest, not even that o⁓⁓⁓⁓ ⁓⁓⁓⁓⁓vation, can make itself felt (p. 41). Nothing about it is premeditated. Though it may desire things passionately, yet this is never so for long, for it is incapable of perseverance. It cannot tolerate any delay between its desire and the fulfilment of what it desires. It has a sense of omnipotence; the notion of impossibility disappears for the individual in a group.[1]

A group is extraordinarily credulous and open to influence, it has no critical faculty, and the improbable does not exist for it. It thinks in images, which call one another up by association (just as they arise with individuals in states of free imagination), and whose agreement with reality is never checked by any reasonable function [*Instanz*].[2] The feelings of a group are always very simple and very exaggerated. So that a group knows neither doubt nor uncertainty.[3]

---

[1] Compare *Totem und Tabu*, III., 'Animismus, Magie, und Allmacht der Gedanken.' [*Totem and Taboo*. New York, Moffat, 1918. London, Kegan Paul, 1919.]

[2] [See footnote p. 69.]

[3] In the interpretation of dreams, to which, indeed, we owe our best knowledge of unconscious mental life, we follow a technical rule of disregarding doubt and uncertainty in the narrative

It goes directly to extremes; if a suspicion is expressed, it is instantly changed into an incontrovertible certainty; a trace of antipathy is turned into furious hatred (p. 56).[1]

Inclined as it itself is to all extremes, a group can only be excited by an excessive stimulus. Anyone who wishes to produce an effect upon it needs no logical adjustment in his arguments; he must paint

---

of the dream, and of treating every element of the, manifest dream as being quite certain. We attribute doubt and uncertainty to the influence of the censorship to which the dream-work is subjected, and we assume that the primary dream-thoughts are not acquainted with doubt and uncertainty as critical processes. They may naturally be present, like everything else, as part of the content of the day's residue which leads to the dream. (See *Die Traumdeutung*, 6. Auflage, 1921, S. 386. [*The Interpretation of Dreams*. Allen and Unwin, 3rd. Edition, 1913, p. 409.])

[1] The same extreme and unmeasured intensification of every emotion is also a feature of the affective life of children, and it is present as well in dream life. Thanks to the isolation of the single emotions in the unconscious, a slight annoyance during the day will express itself in a dream as a wish for the offending person's death, or a breath of temptation may give the impetus to the portrayal in the dream of a criminal action. Hanns Sachs has made an appropriate remark on this point: 'If we try to discover in consciousness all that the dream has made known to us of its bearing upon the present (upon reality), we need not be surprised that what we saw as a monster under the microscope of analysis now reappears as an infusorium.' (*Die Traumdeutung*, S. 457. [Translation p. 493.])

in the most forcible colours, he must exaggerate, and he must repeat the same thing again and again.

Since a group is in no doubt as to what constitutes truth or error, and is conscious, moreover, of its own great strength, it is as intolerant as it is obedient to authority. It respects force and can only be slightly influenced by kindness, which it regards merely as a form of weakness. What it demands of its heroes is strength, or even violence. It wants to be ruled and oppressed and to fear its masters. Fundamentally it is entirely conservative, and it has a deep aversion from all innovations and advances and an unbounded respect for tradition (p. 62).

In order to make a correct judgement upon the morals of groups, one must take into consideration the fact that when individuals come together in a group all their individual inhibitions fall away and all the cruel, brutal and destructive instincts, which lie dormant in individuals as relics of a primitive epoch, are stirred up to find free gratification. But under the influence of suggestion groups are also capable of high achievements in the shape of abnegation, unselfishness, and devotion to an ideal. While with isolated individuals personal interest is almost the only motive force, with groups it is very rarely prominent. It is possible to speak of an individual having his moral standards raised by a group (p. 65). Whereas the intellectual capacity of a group is always far below that of an individual, its ethical conduct may rise as high above his as it may sink deep below it.

Some other features in Le Bon's description show in a clear light how well justified is the identification of the group mind with the mind of primitive people. In groups the most contradictory ideas can exist side by side and tolerate each other, without any conflict arising from the logical contradiction between them. But this is also the case in the unconscious mental life of individuals, of children and of neurotics, as psycho-analysis has long pointed out.[1]

[1] In young children, for instance, ambivalent emotional attitudes towards those who are nearest to them exist side by side for a long time, without either of them interfering with the expression of the other and contrary one. If eventually a conflict breaks out between the two, it is often settled by the child making a change of object and displacing one of the ambivalent emotions on to a substitute. The history of the development of a neurosis in an adult will also show that a suppressed emotion may frequently persist for a long time in unconscious or even in conscious phantasies, the content of which naturally runs directly counter to some predominant tendency, and yet that this antagonism does not result in any proceedings on the part of the ego against what it has repudiated. The phantasy is tolerated for quite a long time, until suddenly one day, usually as a result of an increase in the affective cathexis [see footnote page 48] of the phantasy, a conflict breaks out between it and the ego with all the usual consequences. In the

A group, further, is subject to the truly magical power of words; they can evoke the most formidable tempests in the group mind, and are also capable of stilling them (p. 117). 'Reason and arguments are incapable of combating certain words and formulas. They are uttered with solemnity in the presence of groups, and as soon as they have been pronounced an expression of respect is visible on every countenance, and all heads are bowed. By many they are considered as natural forces, as supernatural powers.' (p. 117.) It is only necessary in this connection to remember the taboo upon names among primitive people and the magical powers which they ascribe to names and words.[1]

And, finally, groups have never thirsted after truth. They demand illusions, and cannot do without

process of a child's development into a mature adult there is a more and more extensive integration of its personality, a co-ordination of the separate instinctive feelings and desires which have grown up in him independently of one another. The analogous process in the domain of sexual life has long been known to us as the co-ordination of all the sexual instincts into a definitive genital organisation. (*Drei Abhandlungen zur Sexualtheorie*, 1905. [*Three Contributions to the Sexual Theory*. Nervous and Mental Disease Monograph Series, No. 7, 1910.]) Moreover, that the unification of the ego is liable to the same interferences as that of the libido is shown by numerous familiar instances, such as that of men of science who have preserved their faith in the Bible, and the like.

[1] See *Totem und Tabu*.

them. They constantly give what is unreal precedence over what is real; they are almost as strongly influenced by what is untrue as by what is true. They have an evident tendency not to distinguish between the two (p. 77).

We have pointed out that this predominance of the life of phantasy and of the illusion born of an unfulfilled wish is the ruling factor in the psychology of neuroses. We have found that what neurotics are guided by is not ordinary objective reality but psychological reality. A hysterical symptom is based upon phantasy instead of upon the repetition of real experience, and the sense of guilt in an obsessional neurosis is based upon the fact of an evil intention which was never carried out. Indeed, just as in dreams and in hypnosis, in the mental operations of a group the function for testing the reality of things falls into the background in comparison with the strength of wishes with their affective cathexis.[1]

What Le Bon says on the subject of leaders of groups is less exhaustive, and does not enable us to make out an underlying principle so clearly. He thinks that as soon as living beings are gathered together in certain numbers, no matter whether they are a herd of animals or a collection of human beings, they place themselves instinctively under the

[1] [See footnote p. 48.]

authority of a chief (p. 134). A group is an obedient herd, which could never live without a master.
It has such a thirst for obedience that it submits
instinctively to anyone who appoints himself its master.

Although in this way the needs of a group carry
it half-way to meet the leader, yet he too must fit in
with it in his personal qualities. He must himself be
held in fascination by a strong faith (in an idea) in
order to awaken the group's faith; he must possess
a strong and imposing will, which the group, which
has no will of its own, can accept from him. Le
Bon then discusses the different kinds of leaders, and
the means by which they work upon the group. On
the whole he believes that the leaders make themselves
felt by means of the ideas in which they themselves
are fanatical believers.

Moreover, he ascribes both to the ideas and to
the leaders a mysterious and irresistible power, which
he calls 'prestige'. Prestige is a sort of domination
exercised over us by an individual, a work or an idea.
It entirely paralyses our critical faculty, and fills us
with astonishment and respect. It would seem to
arouse a feeling like that of fascination in hypnosis
(p. 148). He distinguishes between acquired or artificial and personal prestige. The former is attached
to persons in virtue of their name, fortune and reput-
ation, and to opinions, works of art, etc., in virtue
of tradition. Since in every case it harks back to

the past, it cannot be of much help to us in understanding this puzzling influence. Personal prestige is attached to a few people, who become leaders by means of it, and it has the effect of making every-thing obey them as though by the operation of some magnetic magic. All prestige, however, is also dependent upon success, and is lost in the event of failure (p. 159).

We cannot feel that Le Bon has brought the function of the leader and the importance of prestige completely into harmony with his brilliantly executed picture of the group mind.

III

OTHER ACCOUNTS OF COLLECTIVE
MENTAL LIFE

We have made use of Le Bon's description by
way of introduction, because it fits in so well with
our own Psychology in the emphasis which it lays
upon unconscious mental life. But we must now add
that as a matter of fact none of that author's state-
ments bring forward anything new. Everything that he
says to the detriment and depreciation of the manifestations of the group mind had already been said
by others before him with equal distinctness and
equal hostility, and has been repeated in unison by
thinkers, statesmen and writers since the earliest
periods of literature.[1] The two theses which com-
prise the most important of Le Bon's opinions, those
touching upon the collective inhibition of intellectual
functioning and the heightening of affectivity in groups,

[1] B. Kraškovič jun.: *Die Psychologie der Kollektivitäten.*
Translated [into German] from the Croatian by Siegmund von
Posavec. Vukovar, 1915. See the body of the work as well as
the bibliography.

had been formulated shortly before by Sighele.[1] At bottom, all that is left over as being peculiar to Le Bon are the two notions of the unconscious and of the comparison with the mental life of primitive people, and even these had naturally often been alluded to before him.

But, what is more, the description and estimate of the group mind as they have been given by Le Bon and the rest have not by any means been left undisputed. There is no doubt that all the phenomena of the group mind which have just been mentioned have been correctly observed, but it is also possible to distinguish other manifestations of the group formation, which operate in a precisely opposite sense, and from which a much higher opinion of the group mind must necessarily follow.

Le Bon himself was prepared to admit that in certain circumstances the morals of a group can be higher than those of the individuals that compose it, and that only collectivities are capable of a high degree of unselfishness and devotion. 'While with isolated individuals personal interest is almost the only motive force, with groups it is very rarely prominent.' (p. 65.) Other writers adduce the fact that it is only society which prescribes any ethical

[1] See Walter Moede: 'Die Massen- und Sozialpsychologie im kritischen Überblick.' Meumann and Scheibner's *Zeitschrift für pädagogische Psychologie und experimentelle Pädagogik.* 1915, XVI.

standards at all for the individual, while he as a rule fails in one way or another to come up to its high demands. Or they point out that in exceptional circumstances there may arise in communities the phenomenon of enthusiasm, which has made the most splendid group achievements possible.

As regards intellectual work it remains a fact, indeed, that great decisions in the realm of thought and momentous discoveries and solutions of problems are only possible to an individual, working in solitude. But even the group mind is capable of genius in intellectual creation, as is shown above all by language itself, as well as by folk-song, folk-lore and the like. It remains an open question, moreover, how much the individual thinker or writer owes to the stimulation of the group in which he lives, or whether he does more than perfect a mental work in which the others have had a simultaneous share.

In face of these completely contradictory accounts, it looks as though the work of Group Psychology were bound to come to an ineffectual end. But it is easy to find a more hopeful escape from the dilemma. A number of very different formations have probably been merged under the term 'group' and may require to be distinguished. The assertions of Sighele, Le Bon, and the rest relate to groups of a short-lived character, which some passing interest has hastily agglomerated out of various sorts of individuals.

The characteristics of revolutionary groups, and especially those of the great French Revolution, have unmistakably influenced their descriptions. The opposite opinions owe their origin to the consideration of those stable groups or associations in which mankind pass their lives, and which are embodied in the institutions of society. Groups of the first kind stand in the same sort of relation to those of the second as a high but choppy sea to a ground swell.

McDougall, in his book on *The Group Mind*,[1] starts out from the same contradiction that has just been mentioned, and finds a solution for it in the factor of organisation. In the simplest case, he says, the 'group' possesses no organisation at all or one scarcely deserving the name. He describes a group of this kind as a 'crowd'. But he admits that a crowd of human beings can hardly come together without possessing at all events the rudiments of an organisation, and that precisely in these simple groups many of the fundamental facts of Collective Psychology can be observed with special ease (p. 22). Before the members of a random crowd of people can constitute something in the nature of a group in the psychological sense of the word, a condition has to be fulfilled; these individuals must have something in common with one another, a common interest in

[1] Cambridge University Press, 1920.

an object, a similar emotional bias in some situation or other, and ('consequently', I should like to interpolate) 'some degree of reciprocal influence' (p. 23). The higher the degree of 'this mental homogeneity', the more readily do the individuals form a psychological group, and the more striking are the manifestations of a group mind.

The most remarkable and also the most important result of the formation of a group is the 'exaltation or intensification of emotion' produced in every member of it (p. 24). In McDougall's opinion men's emotions are st..... .... a group to a pitch that they seldom or never attain .... other conditions; and it is a pleasurable expe..... ..e for those who are concerned to surrender themsel..... so unreservedly to their passions and thus to bec..... merged in the group and to lose the sense of the limits of their individuality. The manner in which individuals are thus carried away by a common impulse is explained by McDougall by means of what he calls the 'principle of direct induction of emotion by way of the primitive sympathetic response' (p. 25), that is, by means of the emotional contagion with which we are already familiar. The fact is that the perception of the signs of an emotional state is calculated automatically to arouse the same emotion in the person who perceives them. The greater the number of people in whom the same emotion can be simultaneously observed, the stronger does this automatic compulsion grow. The individual loses his power of criticism, and lets himself slip into the same emotion. But in so doing he increases the excitement of the other people, who had produced this effect upon him, and thus the emotional charge of the individuals becomes intensified by mutual interaction. Something is unmistakably at work in the nature of a compulsion to do the same as the others, to remain in harmony with the many. The coarser and simpler emotions are the more apt to spread through a group in this way (p. 39).

This mechanism for the intensification of emotion is favoured by some other influences which emanate from groups. A group impresses the individual with a sense of unlimited power and of insurmountable peril. For the moment it replaces the whole of human society, which is the wielder of authority, whose punishments the individual fears, and for whose sake he has submitted to so many inhibitions. It is clearly perilous for him to put himself in opposition to it, and it will be safer to follow the example of those around him and perhaps even 'hunt with the pack'. In obedience to the new authority he may put his former 'conscience' out of action, and so surrender to the attraction of the increased pleasure that is certainly obtained from the removal of in-hibitions. On the whole, therefore, it is not so remarkable that we should see an individual in a group doing or approving things which he would have avoided in the normal conditions of life; and in this way we may even hope to clear up a little of the mystery which is so often covered by the enigmatic word 'suggestion'.

McDougall does not dispute the thesis as to the collective inhibition of intelligence in groups (p. 41). He says that the minds of lower intelligence bring down those of a higher order to their own level. The latter are obstructed in their activity, because in general an intensification of emotion creates unfavourable conditions for sound intellectual work, and further because the individuals are intimidated by the group and their mental activity is not free, and because there is a lowering in each individual of his sense of responsibility for his own performances.

The judgement with which McDougall sums up the psychological behaviour of a simple 'unorganised' group is no more friendly than that of Le Bon. Such a group 'is excessively emotional, impulsive, violent, fickle, inconsistent, irresolute and extreme in action, displaying only the coarser emotions and the less refined sentiments; extremely suggestible, careless in deliberation, hasty in judgment, incapable of any but the simpler and imperfect forms of reasoning; easily swayed and led, lacking in self-consciousness, devoid of self-respect and of sense of responsibility, and apt to be carried away by the consciousness of its own force, so that it tends to produce all the manifestations we have learnt to expect of any irresponsible and absolute power. Hence its behaviour is like that of an unruly child or an untutored passionate savage in a strange situation, rather than like that of its average member; and in the worst cases it is like that of a wild beast, rather than like that of human beings.' (p. 45.)

Since McDougall contrasts the behaviour of a highly organised group with what has just been described, we shall be particularly interested to learn in what this organisation consists, and by what factors it is produced. The author enumerates five 'principal conditions' for raising collective mental life to a higher level.

The first and fundamental condition is that there should be some degree of continuity of existence in the group. This may be either material or formal: the former, if the same individuals persist in the group for some time; and the latter, if there is developed within the group a system of fixed positions which are occupied by a succession of individuals.

The second condition is that in the individual member of the group some definite idea should be formed of the nature, composition, functions and capacities of the group, so that from this he may develop an emotional relation to the group as a whole.

The third is that the group should be brought into interaction (perhaps in the form of rivalry) with other groups similar to it but differing from it in many respects.

The fourth is that the group should possess traditions, customs and habits, and especially such as determine the relations of its members to one another.

The fifth is that the group should have a definite structure, expressed in the specialisation and differentiation of the functions of its constituents.

According to McDougall, if these conditions are fulfilled, the psychological disadvantages of the group formation are removed. The collective lowering of intellectual ability is avoided by withdrawing the performance of intellectual tasks from the group and reserving them for individual members of it.

It seems to us that the condition which McDougall designates as the 'organisation' of a group can with more justification be described in another way. The problem consists in how to procure for the group precisely those features which were characteristic of the individual and which are extinguished in him by the formation of the group. For the individual, outside the primitive group, possessed his own continuity, his self-consciousness, his traditions and customs, his own particular functions and position, and kept apart from his rivals. Owing to his entry into an 'unorganised' group he had lost this distinctiveness for a time. If we thus recognise that the aim is to equip the group with the attributes of the individual, we shall be reminded of a valuable remark of Trotter's,[1] to the effect that the tendency towards the formation of groups is biologically a continuation of the multicellular character of all the higher organisms.

[1] *Instincts of the Herd in Peace and War.* Fisher Unwin, 1916.

IV

SUGGESTION AND LIBIDO

We started from the fundamental fact that an individual in a group is subjected through its influence to what is often a profound alteration in his mental activity. His emotions become extraordinarily intensified, while his intellectual ability becomes markedly reduced, both processes being evidently in the direction of an approximation to the other individuals in the group; and this result can only be reached by the removal of those inhibitions upon his instincts which are peculiar to each individual, and by his resigning those expressions of his inclinations which are especially his own. We have heard that these often unwelcome consequences are to some extent at least prevented by a higher 'organisation' of the group; but this does not contradict the fundamental fact of Group Psychology—the two theses as to the intensification of the emotions and the inhibition of the intellect in primitive groups. Our interest is

now directed to discovering the psychological explanation of this mental change which is experienced by
the individual in a group.

It is clear that rational factors (such as the in-
timidation of the individual which has already been
mentioned, that is, the action of his instinct of self-
preservation) do not cover the observable phenomena.
Beyond this what we are offered as an explanation
by authorities upon Sociology and Group Psychology
is always the same, even though it is given various
names, and that is—the magic word 'suggestion'.
Tarde calls it 'imitation'; but we cannot help
agreeing with a writer who protests that imitation
comes under the concept of suggestion, and is in
fact one of its results.[1] Le Bon traces back all the
puzzling features of social phenomena to two factors:
the mutual suggestion of individuals and the prestige
of leaders. But prestige, again, is only recognizable
by its capacity for evoking suggestion. McDougall
for a moment gives us an impression that his principle of 'primitive induction of emotion' might enable
us to do without the assumption of suggestion. But
on further consideration we are forced to perceive
that this principle says no more than the familiar
assertions about 'imitation' or 'contagion', except

---

[1] Brugeilles: 'L'essence du phénomène social: la suggestion.'
Revue philosophique, 1913, XXV.

for a decided stress upon the emotional factor. There is no doubt that something exists in us which, when we become aware of signs of an emotion in someone else, tends to make us fall into the same emotion; but how often do we not successfully oppose it, resist the emotion, and react in quite an opposite way? Why, therefore, do we invariably give way to this contagion when we are in a group? Once more we should have to say that what compels us to obey this tendency is imitation, and what induces the emotion in us is the group's suggestive influence. Moreover, quite apart from this, McDougall does not enable us to evade suggestion; we hear from him as well as from other writers that groups are distinguished by their special suggestibility.

We shall therefore be prepared for the statement that suggestion (or more correctly suggestibility) is actually an irreducible, primitive phenomenon, a fundamental fact in the mental life of man. Such, too, was the opinion of Bernheim, of whose astonishing arts I was a witness in the year 1889. But I can remember even then feeling a muffled hostility to this tyranny of suggestion. When a patient who showed himself unamenable was met with the shout: ' What are you doing? *Vous vous contresuggestionnez!*', I said to myself that this was an evident injustice and an act of violence. For the man certainly had a right to counter-suggestions if they were trying to subdue him with suggestions. Later on my resistance took the direction of protesting against the view that suggestion, which explained everything, was itself to be preserved from explanation. Thinking of it, I repeated the old conundrum :[1]

> Christoph trug Christum,
> Christus trug die ganze Welt,
> Sag' wo hat Christoph
> Damals hin   n Fuss ge   t?[2]

Christophorus Christum, sed Christus sustulit orbem:
   Constiterit pedibus dic ubi Christophorus?

Now that I once more approach the riddle of suggestion after having kept away from it for some thirty years, I find there is no change in the situation. To this statement I can discover only a single exception, which I need not mention, since it is one which bears witness to the influence of psycho-analysis. I notice that particular efforts are being made to formulate the concept of suggestion correctly, that is, to fix the conventional use of the name.[3] And this

[1] Konrad Richter: 'Der deutsche S. Christoph.' Berlin, 1896, *Acta Germanica*, V, 1.

[2] [Literally: 'Christopher bore Christ; Christ bore the whole world; Say, where did Christopher then put his foot?']

[3] Thus, McDougall: 'A Note on Suggestion.' *Journal of Neurology and Psychopathology*, 1920, Vol. I, No. 1.

is by no means superfluous, for the word is acquiring a more and more extended use and a looser and looser meaning, and will soon come to designate any sort of influence whatever, just as in English, where 'to suggest' and 'suggestion' correspond to our *nahelegen* and *Anregung*. But there has been no explanation of the nature of suggestion, that is, of the conditions under which influence without adequate logical foundation takes place. I should not avoid the task of supporting this statement by an analysis of the literature of the last thirty years, if I were not aware that an exhaustive inquiry is being undertaken close at hand which has in view the fulfilment of this very task.

Instead of this I shall make an attempt at using the concept of *libido* for the purpose of throwing light upon Group Psychology, a concept which has done us such good service in the study of psycho-neuroses.

Libido is an expression taken from the theory of the emotions. We call by that name the energy (regarded as a quantitative magnitude, though not at present actually mensurable) of those instincts which have to do with all that may be comprised under the word 'love'. The nucleus of what we mean by love naturally consists (and this is what is commonly called love, and what the poets sing of) in sexual love with sexual union as its aim. But we do not separate from this—what in any case has a share in the name 'love'—on the one hand, self-love, and on the other, love for parents and children, friendship and love for humanity in general, and also devotion to concrete objects and to abstract ideas. Our justification lies in the fact that psycho-analytic research has taught us that all these tendencies are an expression of the same instinctive activities; in relations between the sexes these instincts force their way towards sexual union, but in other circumstances they are diverted from this aim or are prevented from reaching it, though always preserving enough of their original nature to keep their identity recognizable (as in such features as the longing for proximity, and self-sacrifice).

We are of opinion, then, that language has carried out an entirely justifiable piece of unification in creating the word 'love' with its numerous uses, and that we cannot do better than take it as the basis of our scientific discussions and expositions as well. By coming to this decision, psycho-analysis has let loose a storm of indignation, as though it had been guilty of an act of outrageous innovation. Yet psycho-analysis has done nothing original in taking love in this 'wider' sense. In its origin, function, and relation to sexual love, the '*Eros*' of the philosopher Plato coincides exactly with the love force, the libido, of psycho-analysis, as has been shown in detail by

Nachmansohn and Pfister;[1] and when the apostle Paul, in his famous epistle to the Corinthians, prizes love above all else, he certainly understands it in the same 'wider' sense.[2] But this only shows that men do not always take their great thinkers seriously, even when they profess most to admire them.

Psycho-analysis, then, gives these love instincts the name of sexual instincts, *a potiori* and by reason of their origin. The majority of 'educated' people have regarded this nomenclature as an insult, and have taken their revenge by retorting upon psychoanalysis with the reproach of 'pan-sexualism'. Anyone who considers sex as something mortifying and humiliating to human nature is at liberty to make use of the more genteel expressions 'Eros' and 'erotic'. I might have done so myself from the first and thus have spared myself much opposition. But I did not want to, for I like to avoid concessions to faintheartedness. One can never tell where that road may lead one; one gives way first in words, and then little by little in substance too. I cannot see any merit in being ashamed of sex; the Greek word 'Eros',

[1] Nachmansohn: 'Freuds Libidotheorie verglichen mit der Eroslehre Platos'. *Internationale Zeitschrift für Psychoanalyse,* 1915, Bd. III; Pfister: 'Plato als Vorläufer der Psychoanalyse', ibid., 1921, Bd. VII. ['Plato: a Fore-Runner of Psycho-Analysis'. *International Journal of Psycho-Analysis,* 1922, Vol. III.]

[2] 'Though I speak with the tongues of men and of angels, and have not love, I am become as sounding brass, or a tinkling cymbal.'

which is to soften the affront, is in the end nothing more than a translation of our German word *Liebe* [love]; and finally, he who knows how to wait need make no concessions.

We will try our fortune, then, with the supposition that love relationships (or, to use a more neutral expression, emotional ties) also constitute the essence of the group mind. Let us remember that the authorities make no mention of any such relations. What would correspond to them is evidently concealed behind the shelter, the screen, of suggestion. Our hypothesis finds support in the first instance from two passing thoughts. First, that a group is clearly held together by a power of some kind: and to what power could this feat be better ascribed than to Eros, who holds together everything in the world? Secondly, that if an individual gives up his distinctiveness in a group and lets its other members influence him by suggestion, it gives one the impression that he does it because he feels the need of being in harmony with them rather than in opposition to them—so that perhaps after all he does it '*ihnen zu Liebe*'.[1]

---

[1] [An idiom meaning 'for their sake'. Literally: 'for love of them'.—*Translator.*]

V

TWO ARTIFICIAL GROUPS: THE CHURCH AND THE ARMY

We may recall from what we know of the morphology of groups that it is possible to distinguish very different kinds of groups and opposing lines in their development. There are very fleeting groups and extremely lasting ones; homogeneous ones, made up of the same sorts of individuals, and unhomogeneous ones; natural groups, and artificial ones, requiring an external force to keep them together; primitive groups, and highly organised ones with a definite structure. But for reasons which have yet to be explained we should like to lay particular stress upon a distinction to which the authorities have rather given too little attention; I refer to that between leaderless groups and those with leaders. And, in complete opposition to the usual practice, we shall not choose a relatively simple group formation as our point of departure, but shall begin with highly organised, lasting and artificial groups. The most interesting example of such structures are churches—communities of believers—and armies.

A church and an army are artificial groups, that is, a certain external force is employed to prevent them from disintegrating and to check alterations in their structure.   As a rule a person is not consulted, or is given no choice, as to whether he wants to enter such a group; any attempt at leaving it is usually met with persecution or with severe punishment, or has quite definite conditions attached to it. It is quite outside our present interest to enquire why these associations need such special safeguards. We are only attracted by one circumstance, namely that certain facts, which are far more concealed in other cases, can be observed very clearly in those highly organised groups which are protected from dissolution in the manner that has been mentioned.

In a church (and we may with advantage take the Catholic Church as a type) as well as in an army, however different the two may be in other respects, the same illusion holds good of there being a head—in the Catholic Church Christ, in an army its Commander-in-Chief—who loves all the individuals in the group with an equal love.   Everything depends upon this illusion; if it were to be dropped, then both Church and army would dissolve, so far as the external force permitted them to.   This equal love was expressly enunciated by Christ: 'Inasmuch as ye have done it unto one of the least of these my brethren, ye have done it unto me.' He stands to the individual members of the group of believers in the relation of a kind elder brother; he is their father surrogate. All the demands that are made upon the individual are derived from this love of Christ's. A democratic character runs through the Church, for the very reason that before Christ everyone is equal, and that everyone has an equal share in his love. It is not without a deep reason that the similarity between the Christian community and a family ·is invoked, and that believers call themselves brothers in Christ, that is, brothers through the love which Christ has for them. There is no doubt that the tie which unites each individual with Christ is also the cause of the tie which unites them with one another. The like holds good of an army. The Commander-in-Chief is a father who loves all his soldiers equally, and for that reason they are comrades among themselves. The army differs structurally from the Church in being built up of a series of such groups. Every captain is, as it were, the Commander-in-Chief and the father of his company, and so is every non-commissioned officer of his section. It is true that a similar hierarchy has been constructed in the Church, but it does not play the same part in it economically; for more knowledge and care about individuals may be attributed to Christ than to a human Commander-in-Chief.[1]

It is to be noticed that in these two artificial groups each individual is bound by libidinal[2] ties on

[1] An objection will justly be raised against this conception of the libidinal [see next foot-note] structure of an army on the ground that no place has been found in it for such ideas as those of one's country, of national glory, etc., which are of such importance in holding an army together. The answer is that that is a different instance of a group tie, and no longer such a simple one; for the examples of great generals, like Caesar, Wallenstein, or Napoleon, show that such ideas are not indispensable to the existence of an army. We shall presently touch upon the possibility of a leading idea being substituted for a leader and upon the relations between the two. The neglect of this libidinal factor in an army, even when it is not the only factor operative, seems to be not merely a theoretical omission but also a practical danger. Prussian militarism, which was just as unpsychological as German science, may have had to suffer the consequences of this in the great war. We know that the war neuroses which ravaged the German army have been recognized as being a protest of the individual against the part he was expected to play in the army; and according to the communication of E. Simmel (*Kriegsneurosen und 'Psychisches Trauma'*. Munich, 1918), the hard treatment of the men by their superiors may be considered as foremost among the motive forces of the disease. If the importance of the libido's claims on this score had been better appreciated, the fantastic promises of the American President's fourteen points would probably not have been believed so easily, and the splendid instrument would not have broken in the hands of the German leaders.

[2] [Here and elsewhere the German '*libidinös*' is used simply as an adjectival derivative from the technical term '*Libido*';

the one hand to the leader (Christ, the Commander-in-Chief) and on the other hand to the other members of the group. How these two ties are related to each other, whether they are of the same kind and the same value, and how they are to be described psychologically—these questions must be reserved for subsequent enquiry. But we shall venture even now upon a mild reproach against the authorities for not having sufficiently appreciated the importance of the leader in the psychology of the group, while our own choice of a first object for investigation has brought us into a more favourable position. It would appear as though we were on the right road towards an explanation of the principal phenomenon of Group Psychology—the individual's lack of freedom in a group. If each individual is bound in two directions by such an intense emotional tie, we shall find no difficulty in attributing to that circumstance the alteration and limitation which have been observed in his personality.

A hint to the same effect, that the essence of a group lies in the libidinal ties existing in it, is also to be found in the phenomenon of panic, which is best studied in military groups. A panic arises if a group of that kind becomes disintegrated. Its

'libidinal' is accordingly introduced in the translation in order to avoid the highly-coloured connotation of the English 'libidinous'.—*Translator.*]

characteristics are that none of the orders given by superiors are any longer listened to, and that each individual is only solicitous on his own account, and without any consideration for the rest. The mutual ties have ceased to exist, and a gigantic and senseless dread [*Angst*] is set free. At this point, again, the objection will naturally be made that it is rather the other way round; and that the dread has grown so great as to be able to disregard all ties and all feelings of consideration for others. McDougall has even (p. 24) made use of the case of panic (though not of military panic) as a typical instance of that intensification of emotion by contagion ('primary induction') upon which he lays so much emphasis. But nevertheless this rational method of explanation is here quite inadequate. The very question that needs explanation is why the dread has become so gigantic. The greatness of the danger cannot be responsible, for the same army which now falls a victim to panic may previously have faced equally great or greater danger with complete success; it is of the very essence of panic that it bears no relation to the danger that threatens, and often breaks out upon the most trivial occasions. If an individual in panic dread begins to be solicitous only on his own account, he bears witness in so doing to the fact that the emotional ties, which have hitherto made the danger seem small to him, have ceased to exist. Now that he is by himself in facing the danger, he may surely think it greater. The fact is, therefore, that panic dread presupposes a relaxation in the libidinal structure of the group and reacts to it in a justifiable manner, and the contrary view—that the libidinal ties of the group are destroyed owing to dread in the face of the danger—can be refuted.

The contention that dread in a group is increased to enormous proportions by means of induction (contagion) is not in the least contradicted by these remarks. McDougall's view meets the case entirely when the danger is a really great one and when the group has no strong emotional ties—conditions which are fulfilled, for instance, when a fire breaks out in a theatre or a place of amusement. But the really instructive case and the one which can be best employed for our purposes is that mentioned above, in which a body of troops breaks into a panic although the danger has not increased beyond a degree that is usual and has often been previously faced. It is not to be expected that the usage of the word 'panic' should be clearly and unambiguously determined. Sometimes it is used to describe any collective dread, sometimes even dread in an individual when it exceeds all bounds, and often the name seems to be reserved for cases in which the outbreak of dread is not warranted by the occasion. If we take the word 'panic' in the sense of collective dread, we can establish a far-reaching analogy. Dread in an individual is provoked either by the greatness of a danger or by the cessation of emotional ties (libidinal cathexes[1] [*Libidobesetzungen*]); the latter is the case of neurotic dread.[2] In just the same way panic arises either owing to an increase of the common danger or owing to the disappearance of the emotional ties which hold the group together; and the latter case is analogous to that of neurotic dread.[3]

[1] ['Cathexis', from the Greek 'κατέχω', 'I occupy'. The German word '*Besetzung*' has become of fundamental importance in the exposition of psycho-analytical theory. Any attempt at a short definition or description is likely to be misleading, but speaking very loosely, we may say that 'cathexis' is used on the analogy of an electric charge, and that it means the concentration or accumulation of mental energy in some particular channel. Thus, when we speak of the existence in someone of a libidinal cathexis of an object, or, more shortly, of an object-cathexis, we mean that his libidinal energy is directed towards, or rather infused into, the idea (*Vorstellung*) of some object in the outer world. Readers who desire to obtain a more precise knowledge of the term are referred to the discussions in 'Zur Einführung des Narzissmus' and the essays on metapsychology in *Kleine Schriften zur Neurosenlehre*, Vierte. Folge.—*Translator.*]

[2] See *Vorlesungen zur Einführung in die Psychoanalyse.* XXV, 3. Auflage, 1920. [*Introductory Lectures on Psycho-Analysis.* Lecture XXV. George Allen and Unwin, 1922.]

[3] Compare Bela v. Felszeghy's interesting though somewhat fantastic paper 'Panik und Pankomplex'. *Imago,* 1920, Bd. VI.

Anyone who, like McDougall (l. c.), describes a panic as one of the plainest functions of the 'group mind', arrives at the paradoxical position that this group mind does away with itself in one of its most striking manifestations. It is impossible to doubt that panic means the disintegration of a group; it involves the cessation of all the feelings of consideration which the members of the group otherwise show one another.

The typical occasion of the outbreak of a panic is very much as it is represented in Nestroy's parody of Hebbel's play about Judith and Holofernes. A soldier cries out: 'The general has lost his head!' and thereupon all the Assyrians take to flight. The loss of the leader in some sense or other, the birth of misgivings about him, brings on the outbreak of panic, though the danger remains the same; the mutual ties between the members of the group disappear, as a rule, at the same time as the tie with their leader. The group vanishes in dust, like a Bologna flask when its top is broken off.

The dissolution of a religious group is not so easy to observe. A short time ago there came into my hands an English novel of Catholic origin, recommended by the Bishop of London, with the title *When It Was Dark*. It gave a clever and, as it seems to me, a convincing picture of such a possibility and its consequences. The novel, which is supposed to relate to the present day, tells how a conspiracy of enemies of the figure of Christ and of the Christian faith succeed in arranging for a sepulchre to be discovered in Jerusalem. In this sepulchre is an inscription, in which Joseph of Arimathaea confesses that for reasons of piety he secretly removed the body of Christ from its grave on the third day after its entombment and buried it in this spot. The resurrection of Christ and his divine nature are by this means disposed of, and the result of this archaeological discovery is a convulsion in European civilisation and an extraordinary increase in all crimes and acts of violence, which only ceases when the forgers' plot has been revealed.

The phenomenon which accompanies the dissolution that is here supposed to overtake a religious group is not dread, for which the occasion is wanting. Instead of it ruthless and hostile impulses towards other people make their appearance, which, owing to the equal love of Christ, they had previously been unable to do.[1] But even during the kingdom of Christ those people who do not belong to the community of believers, who do not love him, and whom he does not love, stand outside this tie. Therefore

---

[1] Compare the explanation of similar phenomena after the abolition of the paternal authority of the sovereign given in P. Federn's *Die vaterlose Gesellschaft*. Vienna, Anzengruber-Verlag, 1919.

a religion, even if it calls itself the religion of love, must be hard and unloving to those who do not belong to it. Fundamentally indeed every religion is in this same way a religion of love for all those whom it embraces; while cruelty and intolerance towards those who do not belong to it are natural to every religion. However difficult we may find it personally, we ought not to reproach believers too severely on this account; people who are unbelieving or indifferent are so much better off psychologically in this respect. If to-day that intolerance no longer shows itself so violent and cruel as in former centuries, we can scarcely conclude that there has been a softening in human manners. The cause ·is rather to be found in the undeniable weakening of religious feelings and the libidinal ties which depend upon them. If another group tie takes the place of the religious one—and the socialistic tie seems to be succeeding in doing so—, then there will be the same intolerance towards outsiders as in the age of the Wars of Religion; and if differences between scientific opinions could ever attain a similar significance for groups, the same result would again be repeated with this new motivation.

VI

FURTHER PROBLEMS AND LINES OF WORK

We have hitherto considered two artificial groups and have found that they are dominated by two emotional ties. One of these, the tie with the leader, seems (at all events for these cases) to be more of a ruling factor than the other, which holds between the members of the group.

Now much else remains to be examined and described in the morphology of groups. We should have to start from the ascertained fact that a mere collection of people is not a group, so long as these ties have not been established in it; but we should have to admit that in any collection of people the tendency to form a psychological group may very easily become prominent. We should have to give our attention to the different kinds of groups, more or less stable, that arise spontaneously, and to study the conditions of their origin and of their dissolution. We should above all be concerned with the distinction between groups which have a leader and leaderless groups. We should consider whether groups with leaders may not be the more primitive and complete, whether in the others an idea, an abstraction, may not be substituted for the leader (a state of things to which religious groups, with their invisible head, form a transition stage), and whether a common tendency, a wish in which a number of people can have a share, may not in the same way serve as a substitute. This abstraction, again, might be more or less completely embodied in the figure of what we might call a secondary leader, and interesting varieties would arise from the relation between the idea and the leader. The leader or the leading idea might also, so to speak, be negative; hatred against a particular person or institution might operate in just the same unifying way, and might call up the same kind of emotional ties as positive attachment. Then the question would also arise whether a leader is really indispensable to the essence of a group— and other questions besides.

But all these questions, which may, moreover, have been dealt with in part in the literature of Group Psychology, will not succeed in diverting our interest from the fundamental psychological problems that confront us in the structure of a group. And our attention will first be attracted by a consideration which promises to bring us in the most direct way to a proof that libidinal ties are what characterize a group.

Let us keep before our eyes the nature of the emotional relations which hold between men in general. According to Schopenhauer's famous simile of the freezing porcupines no one can tolerate a too intimate approach to his neighbour.[1]

The evidence of psycho-analysis shows that almost every intimate emotional relation between two people which lasts for some time—marriage, friendship, the relations between parents and children[2]—leaves a sediment of feelings of aversion and hostility, which have first to be eliminated by repression. This is less disguised in the common wrangles between business partners or in the grumbles of a subordinate

---

[1] 'A company of porcupines crowded themselves very close together one cold winter's day so as to profit by one another's warmth and so save themselves from being frozen to death. But soon they felt one another's quills, which induced them to separate again. And now, when the need for warmth brought them nearer together again, the second evil arose once more. So that they were driven backwards and forwards from one trouble to the other, until they had discovered a mean distance at which they could most tolerably exist.' (*Parerga und Paralipomena*, II. Teil, XXXI., 'Gleichnisse und Parabeln'.)

[2] Perhaps with the solitary exception of the relation of a mother to her son, which is based upon narcissism, is not disturbed by subsequent rivalry, and is reinforced by a rudimentary attempt at sexual object-choice.

whether community of interest in itself, without any addition of libido, must not necessarily lead to the toleration of other people and to considerateness for them. This objec.... may be met by the reply that nevertheless no lasting limitation of narcissism is effected in this way, since this tolerance does not persist longer than the imn.ediate advantage gained from the other people's collaboration. But the practical importance of the discussion is less than might be supposed, for experience has shown that in cases of collaboration libidinal ties are regularly formed between the fellow-workers which prolong and solidify the relation between them to a point beyond what is merely profitable. The same thing occurs in men's social relations as has become familiar to psycho-analytic research in the course of the development of the individual libido. The libido props itself upon the satisfaction of the great vital needs, and chooses as its first objects the people who have a share in that process. And in the development of mankind as a whole, just as in individuals, love alone acts as the civilizing factor in the sense that it brings a change from egoism to altruism. And this is true both of the sexual love for women, with all the obligations which it involves of sparing what women are fond of, and also of the desexualised, sublimated homosexual love for other men, which springs from work in common.

E

If therefore in groups narcissistic self-love is subject to limitations which do not operate outside them, that is cogent evidence that the essence of a group formation consists in a new kind of libidinal ties among the members of the group.

But our interest now leads us on to the pressing question as to what may be the nature of these ties which exist in groups. In the psycho-analytic study of neuroses we have hitherto been occupied almost exclusively with ties that unite with their objects those love instincts which still pursue directly sexual aims. In groups there can evidently be no question of sexual aims of that kind. We are concerned here with love instincts which have been diverted from their original aims, though they do not operate with less energy on that account. Now we have already observed within the range of the usual sexual object-cathexis [*Objektbesetzung*] phenomena which represent a diversion of the instinct from its sexual aim. We have described them as degrees of being in love, and have recognized that they involve a certain encroachment upon the ego. We shall now turn our attention more closely to these phenomena of being in love, in the firm expectation of finding in them conditions which can be transferred to the ties that exist in groups. But we should also like to know whether this kind of object-cathexis, as we know it in sexual life, represents the only manner of emotional tie with other people, or whether we must take other mechanisms of the sort into account. As a matter of fact we learn from psycho-analysis that there do exist other mechanisms for emotional ties, the so-called *identifications*, insufficiently-known processes and hard to describe, the investigation of which will for some time keep us away from the subject of Group Psychology.

VII

IDENTIFICATION

Identification is known to psycho-analysis as the earliest expression of an emotional tie with another person. It plays a part in the early history of the Oedipus complex. A little boy will exhibit a special interest in his father; he would like to grow like him and be like him, and take his place everywhere. We may say simply that he takes his father as his ideal. This behaviour has nothing to do with a passive or feminine attitude towards his father (and towards males in general); it is on the contrary typically masculine. It fits in very well with the Oedipus complex, for which it helps to prepare the way.

At the same time as this identification with his father, or a little later, the boy has begun to develop a true object-cathexis towards his mother according to the anaclitic type [*Anlehnungstypus*].[1] He then

[1] [Literally, 'leaning-up-against type'; from the Greek 'ἀνακλίνω' 'I lean up against'. In the first phase of their development the

exhibits, therefore, two psychologically distinct ties: a straightforward sexual object-cathexis towards his mother and a typical identification towards his father. The two subsist side by side for a time without any mutual influence or interference. In consequence of the irresistible advance towards a unification of mental life they come together at last; and the normal Oedipus complex originates from their confluence. The little boy notices that his father stands in his way with his mother. His identification with his father then takes on a hostile colouring and becomes identical with the wish to replace his father in regard to his mother as well. Identification, in fact, is ambivalent from the very first; it can turn into an expression of tenderness as easily as into a wish for someone's removal. It behaves like a derivative of the first *oral* phase of the organisation of the libido, in which the object that we long for and prize is assimilated by eating and is in that way annihilated as such. The cannibal, as we know, has remained at

---

sexual instincts have no independent means of finding satisfaction; they do so by propping themselves upon or 'leaning up against' the self-preservative instincts. The individual's first choice of a sexual object is said to be of the 'anaclitic type' when it follows this path; that is, when he choses as his first sexual object the same person who has satisfied his early non-sexual needs. For a full discussion of the anaclitic and narcissistic types of object-choice compare 'Zur Einführung des Narzissmus'.—*Translator*.]

this standpoint; he has a devouring affection for his enemies and only devours people of whom he is fond.[1]

The subsequent history of this identification with the father may easily be lost sight of. It may happen that the Oedipus complex becomes inverted, and that the father is taken as the object of a feminine attitude, an object from which the directly sexual instincts look for satisfaction; in that event the identification with the father has become the precursor of an object tie with the father. The same holds good, with the necessary substitutions, of the baby daughter as well.

It is easy to state in a formula the distinction between an identification with the father and the choice of the father as an object. In the first case one's father is what one would like to *be,* and in the second he is what one would like to *have.* The distinction, that is, depends upon whether the tie attaches to the subject or to the object of the ego. The former is therefore already possible before any sexual object-choice has been made. It is much more

[1] See *Drei Abhandlungen zur Sexualtheorie,* and Abraham's 'Untersuchungen über die früheste prägenitale Entwicklungsstufe der Libido', *Internationale Zeitschrift für Psychoanalyse,* 1916, Bd. IV; also included in his *Klinische Beiträge zur Psychoanalyse* (Internationale psychoanalytische Bibliothek. Nr. 10, 1921).

difficult to give a clear metapsychological representation of the distinction. We can only see that
identification endeavours to mould a person's own
ego after the fashion of the one that has been taken
as a 'model'.

Let us disentangle identification as it occurs in
the structure of a neurotic symptom from its rather
complicated connections. Supposing that a little girl
(and we will keep to her for the present) develops
the same painful symptom as her mother—for instance,
the same tormenting cough. Now this may come
about in various ways. The identification may come
from the Oedipus complex; in that case it signifies
a hostile desire on the girl's part to take her
mother's place, and the symptom expresses her
object love towards her father, and brings about
a realisation, under the influence of a sense of
guilt, of her desire to take her mother's place:
'You wanted to be your mother, and now you
are—anyhow as far as the pain goes'. This is
the complete mechanism of the structure of a
hysterical symptom. Or, on the other hand, the
symptom may be the same as that of the person
who is loved—(so, for instance, Dora in the
'Bruchstück einer Hysterieanalyse'[1] imitated her
father's cough); in that case we can only describe

---

[1] [*Kleine Schriften zur Neurosenlehre.* Zweite Folge.]

the state of things by saying that *identification has appeared instead of object-choice, and that object-choice has regressed to identification.* We have heard that identification is the earliest and original form of emotional tie; it often happens that under the conditions in which symptoms are constructed, that is, where there is repression and where the mechanisms of the unconscious are dominant, object-choice is turned back into identification—the ego, that is, assumes the characteristics of the object. It is noticeable that in these identifications the ego sometimes copies the person who is not loved and sometimes the one who is loved. It must also strike us that in both cases the identification is a partial and extremely limited one and only borrows a single trait from the person who is its object.

There is a third particularly frequent and important case of symptom formation, in which the identification leaves any object relation to the person who is being copied entirely out of account. Supposing, for instance, that one of the girls in a boarding school has had a letter from someone with whom she is secretly in love which arouses her jealousy, and that she reacts to it with a fit of hysterics; then some of her friends who know about it will contract the fit, as we say, by means of mental infection. The mechanism is that of identification based upon the possibility or desire of putting oneself in the same situation. The other girls would like to have a secret love affair too, and under the influence of a sense of guilt they also accept the pain involved in it. It would be wrong to suppose that they take on the symptom out of sympathy. On the contrary, the sympathy only arises out of the identification, and this is proved by the fact that infection or imitation of this kind takes place in circumstances where even less pre-existing sympathy is to be assumed than usually exists between friends in a girls' school. One ego has perceived a significant analogy with another upon one point—in our example upon a similar readiness for emotion; an identification is thereupon constructed on this point, and, under the influence of the pathogenic situation, is displaced on to the symptom which the one ego has produced. The identification by means of the symptom has thus become the mark of a point of coincidence between the two egos which has to be kept repressed.

What we have learned from these three sources may be summarised as follows. First, identification is the original form of emotional tie with an object; secondly, in a regressive way it becomes a substitute for a libidinal object tie, as it were by means of the introjection of the object into the ego; and thirdly, it may arise with every new perception of a common quality shared with some other person who is not an object of the sexual instinct. The more important this common quality is, the more successful may this partial identification become, and it may thus represent the beginning of a new tie.

We already begin to divine that the mutual tie between members of a group is in the nature of an identification of this kind, based upon an important emotional common quality; and we may suspect that this common quality lies in the nature of the tie with the leader. Another suspicion may tell us that we are far from having exhausted the problem of identification, and that we are faced by the process which psychology calls ' empathy [*Einfühlung*] ' and which plays the largest part in our understanding of what is inherently foreign to our ego in other people. But we shall here limit ourselves to the immediate emotional effects of identification, and shall leave on one side its significance for our intellectual life.

Psycho-analytic research, which has already occasionally attacked the more difficult problems of the psychoses, has also been able to exhibit identification to us in some other cases which are not immediately comprehensible. I shall treat two of these cases in detail as material for our further consideration.

The genesis of male homosexuality in a large class of cases is as follows. A young man has been unusually long and intensely fixated upon his mother in the sense of the Oedipus complex. But

at last, after the end of his puberty, the time comes
for exchanging his mother for some other sexual
object. Things take a sudden turn: the young man
does not abandon his mother, but identifies himself
with her; he transforms himself into her, and now
looks about for objects which can replace his ego
for him, and on which he can bestow such love and
care as he has experienced from his mother. This is
a frequent process, which can be confirmed as often
as one likes, and which is naturally quite independent
of any hypothesis that may be made as to the organic driving force and the motives of the sudden
transformation. A striking thing about this identification is its ample scale; it remoulds the ego in one
of its important features—in its sexual character—
upon the model of what has hitherto been the object.
In this process the object itself is renounced—whether
entirely or in the sense of being preserved only in
the unconscious is a question outside the present
discussion. Identification with an object that is renounced or lost as a substitute for it, introjection of
this object into the ego, is indeed no longer a novelty
to us. A process of the kind may sometimes be
directly observed in small children. A short time
ago an observation of this sort was published in the
Internationale Zeitschrift für Psychoanalyse. A child
who was unhappy over the loss of a kitten declared
straight out that now he himself was the kitten, and

accordingly crawled about on all fours, would not eat at table, etc.[1]

Another such instance of introjection of the object has been provided by the analysis of melancholia, an affection which counts among the most remarkable of its exciting causes the real or emotional loss of a loved object. A leading characteristic of these cases is a cruel self-depreciation of the ego combined with relentless self-criticism and bitter self-reproaches. Analyses have shown that this disparagement and these reproaches apply at bottom to the object and represent the ego's revenge upon it. The shadow of the object has fallen upon the ego, as I have said elsewhere.[2] The introjection of the object is here unmistakably clear.

But these melancholias also show us something else, which may be of importance for our later discussions. They show us the ego divided, fallen into two pieces, one of which rages against the second. This second piece is the one which has been altered by introjection and which contains the lost object. But the piece which behaves so cruelly is not unknown to us either. It comprises the conscience, a

---

[1] Marcuszewicz: 'Beitrag zum autistischen Denken bei Kindern.' *Internationale Zeitschrift für Psychoanalyse,* 1920, Bd. VI.

[2] ['Trauer und Melancholie.' *Kleine Schriften zur Neurosenlehre,* Vierte Folge, 1918.]

critical faculty [*Instanz*][1] within the ego, which even
in normal times takes up a critical attitude towards
the ego, though never so relentlessly and so unjusti-
fiably. On previous occasions we have been driven to
the hypothesis[2] that some such faculty develops in
our ego which may cut itself off from the rest of
the ego and come into conflict with it. We have
called it the 'ego ideal', and by way of functions
we have ascribed to it self-observation, the moral
conscience, the censorship of dreams, and the chief
influence in repression. We have said that it is the
heir to the original narcissism in which the childish
ego found its self-sufficiency; it gradually gathers up
from the influences of the environment the demands
which that environment makes upon the ego and
which the ego cannot always rise to; so that a man,
when he cannot be satisfied with his ego itself, may
nevertheless be able to find satisfaction in the ego
ideal which has been differentiated out of the ego.
In delusions of observation, as we have further shown,
the disintegration of this faculty has become patent,
and has thus revealed its origin in the influence of

---

[1] ['*Instanz*'—like 'instance' in the phrase 'court of first
instance'—was originally a legal term. It is now used in the sense
of one of a hierarchy of authorities or functions.—*Translator.*]

[2] 'Zur Einführung des Narzissmus', 'Trauer und Melancholie'.

superior powers, and above all of parents.[1] But we have not forgotten to add that the amount of distance between this ego ideal and the real ego is very variable from one individual to another, and that with many people this differentiation within the ego does not go further than with children.

But before we can employ this material for understanding the libidinal organisation of groups, we must take into account some other examples of the mutual relations between the object and the ego.[2]

---

[1] 'Zur Einführung des Narzissmus.'

[2] We are very well aware that we have not exhausted the nature of identification with these examples taken from pathology, and that we have consequently left part of the riddle of group formations untouched. A far more fundamental and comprehensive psychological analysis would have to intervene at this point. A path leads from identification by way of imitation to empathy, that is, to the comprehension of the mechanism by means of which we are enabled to take up any attitude at all towards another mental life. Moreover there is still much to be explained in the manifestations of existing identifications. These result among other things in a person limiting his aggressiveness towards those with whom he has identified himself, and in his sparing them and giving them help. The study of such identifications, like those, for instance, which lie at the root of clan feeling, led Robertson Smith to the surprising result that they rest upon the recognition of a common substance (*Kinship and Marriage*, 1885), and may even therefore be brought about by a meal eaten in common. This feature makes it possible to connect this kind of identification with the early history of the human family which I constructed in *Totem und Tabu*.

VIII

BEING IN LOVE AND HYPNOSIS

Even in its caprices the usage of language remains true to some kind of reality. Thus it gives the name of 'love' to a great many kinds of emotional relationship which we too group together theoretically as love; but then again it feels a doubt whether this love is real, true, actual love, and so hints at a whole scale of possibilities within the range of the phenomena of love. We shall have no difficulty in making the same discovery empirically.

In one class of cases being in love is nothing more than object-cathexis on the part of the sexual instincts with a view to directly sexual satisfaction, a cathexis which expires, moreover, when this aim has been reached; this is what is called common, sensual love. But, as we know, the libidinal situation rarely remains so simple. It was possible to calculate with certainty upon the revival of the need which had just expired; and this must no doubt have been the first motive for directing a lasting cathexis upon the sexual object and for 'loving' it in the passionless intervals as well.

To this must be added another factor derived from the astonishing course of development which is pursued by the erotic life of man. In his first phase, which has usually come to an end by the time he is five years old, a child has found the first object for his love in one or other of his parents, and all of his sexual instincts with their demand for satisfactio have been united upon this object. The repression which then sets in compels him to renounce the greater number of these infantile sexual aims, and leaves behind a profound modification in his relation to his parents. The child still remains tied to his parents, but by instincts which must be described as being 'inhibited in their aim [*zielgehemmte*]'. The emotions which he feels henceforward towards these objects of his love are characterized as 'tender'. It is well known that the earlier 'sensual' tendencies remain more or less strongly preserved in the unconscious, so that in a certain sense the whole of the original current continues to exist.[1]

At puberty, as we know, there set in new and very strong tendencies with directly sexual aims. In unfavourable cases they remain separate, in the form

[1] Cf. *Drei Abhandlungen zur Sexualtheorie*, l.c.

of a sensual current, from the 'tender' emotional trends which persist. We are then faced by a picture the two aspects of which certain movements in literature take such delight in idealising. A man of this kind will show a sentimental enthusiasm for women whom he deeply respects but who do not excite him to sexual activities, and he will only be potent with other women whom he does not 'love' but thinks little of or even despises.[1] More often, however, the adolescent succeeds in bringing about a certain degree of synthesis between the unsensual, heavenly love and the sensual, earthly love, and his relation to his sexual object is characterised by the interaction of uninhibited instincts and of instincts inhibited in their aim. The depth to which anyone is in love, as contrasted with his purely sensual desire, may be measured by the size of the share taken by the inhibited instincts of tenderness.

In connection with this question of being in love we have always been struck by the phenomenon of sexual over-estimation—the fact that the loved object enjoys a certain amount of freedom from criticism, and that all its characteristics are valued more highly than those of people who are not loved, or than its own were at a time when it itself was not loved. If the sensual

[1] 'Über die allgemeinste Erniedrigung des Liebeslebens.' *Kleine Schriften zur Neurosenlehre*, Vierte Folge, 1918.

F

tendencies are somewhat more effectively repressed or set aside, the illusion is produced that the object has come to be sensually loved on account of its spiritual merits, whereas on the contrary these merits may really only have been lent to it by its sensual charm.

The tendency which falsifies judgement in this respect is that of *idealisation*. But this makes it easier for us to find our way about. We see that the object is being treated in the same way as our own ego, so that when we are in love a considerable amount of narcissistic libido overflows on to the object. It is even obvious, in many forms of love choice, that the object serves as a substitute for some unattained ego ideal of our own. We love it on account of the perfections which we have striven to reach for our own ego, and which we should now like to procure in this roundabout way as a means of satisfying our narcissism.

If the sexual over-estimation and the being in love increase even further, then the interpretation of the picture becomes still more unmistakable. The tendencies whose trend is towards directly sexual satisfaction may now be pushed back entirely, as regularly happens, for instance, with the young man's sentimental passion; the ego becomes more and more unassuming and modest, and the object more and more sublime and precious, until at last it gets possession of the entire self-love of the ego, whose self-sacrifice thus follows as a natural consequence. The object has, so to speak, consumed the ego. Traits of humility, of the limitation of narcissism, and of self-injury occur in every case of being in love; in the extreme case they are only intensified, and as a result of the withdrawal of the sensual claims they remain in solitary supremacy.

This happens especially easily with love that is unhappy and cannot be satisfied; for in spite of everything each sexual satisfaction always involves a reduction in sexual over-estimation. Contemporaneously with this ' devotion ' of the ego to the object, which is no longer to be distinguished from a sublimated devotion to an abstract idea, the functions allotted to the ego ideal entirely cease to operate. The criticism exercised by that faculty is silent; everything that the object does and asks for is right and blameless. Conscience has no application to anything that is done for the sake of the object; in the blindness of love remorselessness is carried to the pitch of crime. The whole situation can be completely summarised in a formula: *The object has taken the place of the ego ideal.*

It is now easy to define the distinction between identification and such extreme developments of being in love as may be described as fascination or infatuation. In the former case the ego has enriched itself with the properties of the object, it has 'introjected' the object into itself, as Ferenczi expresses it. In the second case it is impoverished, it has surrendered itself to the object, it has substituted the object for its most important constituent. Closer consideration soon makes it plain, however, that this kind of account creates an illusion of contradistinctions that have no real existence. Economically ~e is no question of impoverishment or enrichment, '~ even possible to describe an extreme case of being in love as a state in which the ego has introjected the object into itself. Another distinction is perhaps better calculated to meet the essence of the matter. In the case of identification the object has been lost or given up; it is then set up again inside the ego, and the ego makes a partial alteration in itself after the model of the lost object. In the other case the object is retained, and there is a hyper-cathexis of it by the ego and at the ego's expense. But here again a difficulty presents itself. Is it quite certain that identification presupposes that object-cathexis has been given up? Can there be no identification with the object retained? And before we embark upon a discussion of this delicate question, the perception may already be beginning to dawn on us that yet another alternative embraces the real essence of the matter, namely, *whether the object is put in the place of the ego or of the ego ideal.*

From being in love to hypnosis is evidently only a short step. The respects in which the two agree are obvious. There is the same humble subjection, the same compliance, the same absence of criticism, towards the hypnotist just as towards the loved object. There is the same absorption of one's own initiative; no one can doubt that the hypnotist has stepped into the place of the ego ideal. It is only that everything is even clearer and more intense in hypnosis, so that it would be more to the point to explain being in love by means of hypnosis than the other way round. The hypnotist is the sole object, and no attention is paid to any but him. The fact that the ego experiences in a dream-like way whatever he may request or assert reminds us that we omitted to mention among the functions of the ego ideal the business of testing the reality of things.[1] No wonder that the ego takes a perception for real if its reality is vouched for by the mental faculty which ordinarily discharges the duty of testing the reality of things. The complete absence of tendencies which are uninhibited in their sexual aims contributes further towards the extreme purity of the phenomena. The hypnotic relation is the devotion of someone in love to an unlimited degree but with sexual satisfaction excluded;

[1] Cf. 'Metapsychologische Ergänzung zur Traumlehre.' *Kleine Schriften zur Neurosenlehre*, Vierte Folge, 1918.

whereas in the case of being in love this kind of satisfaction is only temporarily kept back, and remains in the background as a possible aim at some later time.

But on the other hand we may also say that the hypnotic relation is (if the expression is permissible) a group formation with two members. Hypnosis is not a good object for comparison with a group formation, because it is truer to say that it is identical with it. Out of the complicated fabric of the group it isolates one element for us—the behaviour of the individual to the leader. Hypnosis is distinguished from a group formation by this limitation of number, just as it is distinguished from being in love by the absence of directly sexual tendencies. In this respect it occupies a middle position between the two.

It is interesting to see that it is precisely those sexual tendencies that are inhibited in their aims which achieve such lasting ties between men. But this can easily be understood from the fact that they are not capable of complete satisfaction, while sexual tendencies which are uninhibited in their aims suffer an extraordinary reduction through the discharge of energy every time the sexual aim is attained. It is the fate of sensual love to become extinguished when it is satisfied; for it to be able to last, it must from the first be mixed with purely tender components—with such, that is, as are inhibited in their aims—or it must itself undergo a transformation of this kind.

Hypnosis would solve the riddle of the libidinal constitution of groups for us straight away, if it were not that it itself exhibits some features which are not met by the rational explanation we have hitherto given of it as a state of being in love with the directly sexual tendencies excluded. There is still a great deal in it which we must recognise as unexplained and mystical. It contains an additional element of paralysis derived from the relation between someone with superior power and someone who is without power and helpless—which may afford a transition to the hypnosis of terror which occurs in animals. The manner in which it is produced and its relationship to sleep are not clear; and the puzzling way in which some people are subject to it, while others resist it completely, points to some factor still unknown which is realised in it and which perhaps alone makes possible the purity of the attitudes of the libido which it exhibits. It is noticeable that, even when there is complete suggestive compliance in other respects, the moral conscience of the person hypnotized may show resistance. But this may be due to the fact that in hypnosis as it is usually practised some knowledge may be retained that what is happening is only a game, an untrue reproduction of another situation of far more importance to life.

But after the preceding discussions we are quite in a position to give the formula for the libidinal

constitution of groups: or at least of such groups as
we have hitherto considered, namely, those that have
a leader and have not been able by means of too much
'organisation' to acquire secondarily the characteristics
of an individual. *A primary group of this kind is
a number of individuals who have substituted one and
the same object for their ego ideal and have consequently identified themselves with one another in their
ego.* This condition admits of graphic representation:

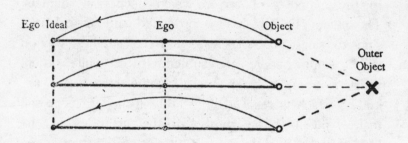

IX

THE HERD INSTINCT

We cannot for long enjoy the illusion that we have solved the riddle of the group with this formula. It is impossible to escape the immediate and disturbing recollection that all we have really done has been to shift the question on to the riddle of hypnosis, about which so many points have yet to be cleared up. And now another objection shows us our further path.

It might be said that the intense emotional ties which we observe in groups are quite sufficient to explain one of their characteristics—the lack of independence and initiative in their members, the similarity in the reactions of all of them, their reduction, so to speak, to the level of group individuals. But if we look at it as a whole, a group shows us more than this. Some of its features—the weakness of intellectual ability, the lack of emotional restraint, the incapacity for moderation and delay, the inclination to exceed every limit in the expression of emotion and to work it off completely in the form of action—these and similar features, which we find so impressively described in Le Bon, show an unmistakable picture of a regression of mental activity to an earlier stage such as we are not surprised to find among savages or children. A regression of this sort is in particular an essential characteristic of common groups, while, as we have heard, in organized and artificial groups it can to a large extent be checked.

We thus have an impression of a state in which an individual's separate emotion and personal intellectual act are too weak to come to anything by themselves and are absolutely obliged to wait till they are reinforced through being repeated in a similar way in the other members of the group. We are reminded of how many of these phenomena of dependence are part of the normal constitution of human society, of how little originality and personal courage are to be found in it, of how much every individual is ruled by those attitudes of the group mind which exhibit themselves in such forms as racial characteristics, class prejudices, public opinion, etc. The influence of suggestion becomes a greater riddle for us when we admit that it is not exercised only by the leader, but by every individual upon every other individual; and we must reproach ourselves with having unfairly emphasized the relation to the leader and with having kept the other factor of mutual suggestion too much in the background.

After this encouragement to modesty, we shall
be inclined to listen to another voice, which promises
us an explanation based upon simpler grounds. Such
a one is to be found in Trotter's thoughtful book
upon the herd instinct, concerning which my only regret
is that it does not entirely escape the antipathies that
were set loose by the recent great war.[1]

Trotter derives the mental phenomena that are
described as occurring in groups from a herd instinct
('gregariousness'), which is innate in human beings just
as in other species of animals. Biologically this gregariousness is an analogy to multicellularity and as
it were a continuation of it. From the standpoint of
the libido theory it is a further manifestation of the
inclination, which proceeds from the libido, and which
is felt by all living beings of the same kind, to combine
in more and more comprehensive units.[2] The individual
feels 'incomplete' if he is alone. The dread shown
by small children would seem already to be an expression of this herd instinct. Opposition to the herd
is as good as separation from it, and is therefore
anxiously avoided. But the herd turns away from
anything that is new or unusual. The herd instinct

---

[1] W. Trotter: *Instincts of the Herd in Peace and War.*
Fisher Unwin, 1916.

[2] See my essay *Jenseits des Lustprinzips.*

would appear to be something primary, something 'which cannot be split up'.

Trotter gives as the list of instincts which he considers as primary those of self-preservation, of nutrition, of sex, and of the herd. The last often comes into opposition with the others. The feelings of guilt and of duty are the peculiar possessions of a gregarious animal. Trotter also derives from the herd instinct the repressive force which psycho-analysis has shown to exist in the ego, and from the same source accordingly the resistances which the physician comes up against in psycho-analytic treatment. Speech owes its importance to its aptitude for mutual understanding in the herd, and upon it the identification of the individuals with one another largely rests.

While Le Bon is principally concerned with typical transient group formations, and McDougall with stable associations, Trotter has chosen as the centre of his interest the most generalised form of assemblage in which man, that ζῷον πολιτικόν, passes his life, and he gives us its psychological basis. But Trotter is under no necessity of tracing back the herd instinct, for he characterizes it as primary and not further reducible. Boris Sidis's attempt, to which he refers, at tracing the herd instinct back to suggestibility is fortunately superfluous as far as he is concerned; it is an explanation of a familiar and unsatisfactory type, and the converse proposition—that suggestibility is a derivative of the herd instinct—would seem to me to throw far more light on the subject.

But Trotter's exposition, with even more justice than the others', is open to the objection that it takes too little account of the leader's part in a group, while we incline rather to the opposite judgement, that it is impossible to grasp the nature of a group if the leader is disregarded. Th   leaves no room at all for the leader; he is merely   along with the herd, almost by chance; it follows, too, that no path leads from this instinct to the need for a God; the herd is without a herdsman. But besides this Trotter's exposition can be undermined psychologically; that is to say, it can be made at all events probable that the herd instinct is not irreducible, that it is not primary in the same sense as the instinct of self-preservation and the sexual instinct.

It is naturally no easy matter to trace the ontogenesis of the herd instinct. The dread which is shown by small children when they are left alone, and which Trotter claims as being already a manifestation of the instinct, nevertheless suggests more readily another interpretation. The dread relates to the child's mother, and later to other familiar persons, and it is the expression of an unfulfilled desire, which the child does not yet know how to deal with in any way except by turning it into dread.[1] Nor is the child's dread when it is alone pacified by the sight of any haphazard ' member of the herd ', but on the contrary it is only brought into existence by the approach of a ' stranger ' of this sort. Then for a long time nothing in the nature of herd instinct or group feeling is to be observed in children. Something like it grows up first of all, in a nursery containing many children, out of the children's relation to their parents, and it does so as a reaction to the initial envy with which the elder child receives the younger one. The elder child would certainly like to put its successor jealously aside, to keep it away from the parents, and to rob it of all its privileges; but in face of the fact that this child (like all that come later) is loved by the parents in just the same way, and in consequence of the impossibility of maintaining its hostile attitude without damaging itself, it is forced into identifying itself with the other children. So there grows up in the troop of children a communal or group feeling, which is then further developed at school. The first demand made by this reaction-formation is for justice, for equal treatment for all. We all know how loudly and implacably this claim is put forward at school. If one cannot be the favourite oneself, at all events nobody else

---

[1] See the remarks upon Dread in *Vorlesungen zur Einführung in die Psychoanalyse*. XXV.

shall be the favourite. This transformation—the replacing of jealousy by a group feeling in the nursery and classroom—might be considered improbable, if the same process could not later on be observed again in other circumstances. We have only to think of the troop of women and girls, all of them in love in an enthusiastically sentimental way, who crowd round a singer or pianist after his performance. It would certainly be easy for each of them to be jealous of the rest; but, in face of their numbers and the consequent impossibility of their reaching the aim of their love, they renounce it, and, instead of pulling out one another's hair, they act as a united group, do homage to the hero of the occasion with their common actions, and would probably be glad to have a share of his flowing locks. Originally rivals, they have succeeded in identifying themselves with one another by means of a similar love for the same object. When, as is usual, a situation in the field of the instincts is capable of various outcomes, we need not be surprised if the actual outcome is one which involves the possibility of a certain amount of satisfaction, while another, even though in itself more obvious, is passed over because the circumstances of life prevent its attaining this aim.

What appears later on in society in the shape of *Gemeingeist*, *esprit de corps*, 'group spirit', etc., does not belie its derivation from what was originally envy. No one must want to put himself forward, every one must be the same and have the same. Social justice means that we deny ourselves many things so that others may have to do without them as well, or, what is the same thing, may not be able to ask for them. This demand for equality is the root of social conscience and the sense of duty. It reveals itself unexpectedly in the syphilitic's dread of infecting other people, which psycho-analysis has taught us to understand. The dread exhibited by these poor wretches corresponds to their violent struggles against the unconscious wish to spread their infection on to other people; for why should they alone be infected and cut off from so much? why not other people as well? And the same germ is to be found in the pretty anecdote of the judgement of Solomon. If one woman's child is dead, the other shall not have a live one either. The bereaved woman is recognized by this wish.

Thus social feeling is based upon the reversal of what was first a hostile feeling into a positively-toned tie of the nature of an identification. So far as we have hitherto been able to follow the course of events, this reversal appears to be effected under the influence of a common tender tie with a person outside the group. We do not ourselves regard our analysis of identification as exhaustive, but it is enough for our present purpose that we should revert to this one

feature—its demand that equalization shall be con-
sistently carried through. We have already heard in
the discussion of the two artificial groups, church and
army, that their preliminary condition is that all their
members should be loved in the same way by one
person, the leader. Do not let us forget, however, that
the demand for equality in a group applies only to its
members and not to the leader. All the members
must be equal to one another, but they all want to
be ruled by one person. Many equals, who can
identify themselves with one another, and a single
person superior to them all—that is the situation
that we find realised in groups which are capable of
subsisting. Let us venture, then, to correct Trotter's
pronouncement that man is a herd animal and assert
that he is rather a horde animal, an individual creature
in a horde led by a chief.

G

X

THE GROUP AND THE PRIMAL HORDE

In 1912 I took up a conjecture of Darwin's to the effect that the primitive form of human society was that of a horde ruled over despotically by a powerful male. I attempted to show that the fortunes of this horde have left indestructible traces upon the history of human descent; and, especially, that the development of totemism, which comprises in itself the beginnings of religion, morality, and social organisation, is connected with the killing of the chief by violence and the transformation of the paternal horde into a community of brothers.[1] To be sure, this is only a hypothesis, like so many others with which archaeologists endeavour to lighten the darkness of prehistoric times—a 'Just-So Story', as it was amusingly called by a not unkind critic (Kroeger); but I think it is creditable to such a hypothesis if it proves able to

[1] *Totem und Tabu.*

bring coherence and understanding into more and more new regions.

Human groups exhibit once again the familiar picture of an individual of superior strength among a troop of similar companions, a picture which is also contained in our idea of the primal horde. The psychology of such a group, as we know it from the descriptions to which we have so often referred—the dwindling of the conscious individual personality, the focussing of thoughts and feelings into a common direction, the predominance of the emotions and of the unconscious mental life, the tendency to the immediate carrying out of intentions as they emerge—all this corresponds to a state of regression to a primitive mental activity, of just such a sort as we should be inclined to ascribe to the primal horde.[1]

---

[1] What we have just described in our general characterisation of mankind must apply especially to the primal horde. The will of the individual was too weak; he did not venture upon action. No impulses whatever came into play except collective ones; there was only a common will, there were no single ones. An idea did not dare to turn itself into a volition unless it felt itself reinforced by a perception of its general diffusion. This weakness of the idea is to be explained by the strength of the emotional tie which is shared by all the members of the horde; but the similarity in the circumstances of their life and the absence of any private property assist in determining the uniformity of their individual mental acts. As we may observe with children and soldiers, common activity is not excluded even in the excremental functions. The one great exception is provided by the

Thus the group appears to us as a revival of the primal horde. Just as primitive man virtually survives in every individual, so the primal horde may arise once more out of any random crowd; in so far as men are habitually under the sway of group formation we recognise in it the survival of the primal horde. We must conclude that the psychology of the group is the oldest human psychology; what we have isolated as individual psychology, by neglecting all traces of the group, has only since come into prominence out of the old group psychology, by a gradual process which may still, perhaps, be described as incomplete. We shall later venture upon an attempt at specifying the point of departure of this development.

Further reflection will show us in what respect this statement requires correction. Individual psychology must, on the contrary, be just as old as group psychology, for from the first there were two kinds of psychologies, that of the individual members of the group and that of the father, chief, or leader. The members of the group were subject to ties just as we see them to-day, but the father of the primal horde was free. His intellectual acts were strong and

sexual act, in which a third person is at the best superfluous and in the extreme case is condemned to a state of painful expectancy. As to the reaction of the sexual need (for genital gratification) towards gregariousness, see below.

independent even in isolation, and his will needed no reinforcement from others. Consistency leads us to assume that his ego had few libidinal ties; he loved no one but himself, or other people only in so far as they served his needs. To objects his ego gave away no more than was barely necessary.

He, at the very beginning of the history of mankind, was the *Superman* whom Nietzsche only expected from the future. Even to-day the members of a group stand in need of the illusion that they are equally and justly loved by their leader; but the leader himself need love no one else, he may be of a masterly nature, absolutely narcissistic, but self-confident and independent. We know that love puts a check upon narcissism, and it would be possible to show how, by operating in this way, it became a factor of civilisation.

The primal father of the horde was not yet immortal, as he later became by deification. If he died, he had to be replaced; his place was probably taken by a youngest son, who had up to then been a member of the group like any other. There must therefore be a possibility of transforming group psychology into individual psychology; a condition must be discovered under which such a transformation is easily accomplished, just as it is possible for bees in case of necessity to turn a larva into a queen instead of into a worker. One can imagine only one possibility:

the primal father had prevented his sons from satisfying their directly sexual tendencies; he forced them
into abstinence and consequently into the emotional
ties with him and with one another which could arise
out of those of their tendencies that were inhibited
in their sexual aim. He forced them, so to speak,
into group psychology. His sexual jealousy and intolerance became in the last resort the causes of group
psychology.[1]

Whoever became his successor was also given
the possibility of sexual satisfaction, and was by that
means offered a way out of the conditions of group
psychology. The fixation of the libido to woman and
the possibility of satisfaction without any need for delay
or accumulation made an end of the importance of
those of his sexual tendencies that were inhibited in
their aim, and allowed his narcissism always to rise
to its full height. We shall return in a postscript to
this connection between love and character formation.

We may further emphasize, as being specially
instructive, the relation that holds between the contrivance by means of which an artificial group is held
together and the constitution of the primal horde.
We have seen that with an army and a church this

[1] It may perhaps also be assumed that the sons, when they
were driven out and separated from their father, advanced from
identification with one another to homosexual object love, and in
this way won freedom to kill their father.

contrivance is the illusion that the leader loves all of the individuals equally and justly. But this is simply an idealistic remodelling of the state of affairs in the primal horde, where all of the sons knew that they were equally persecuted by the primal father, and feared him equally. This same recasting upon which all social duties are built up is already presupposed by the next form of human society, the totemistic clan. The indestructible strength of the family as a natural group formation rests upon the fact that this necessary presupposition of the father's equal love can have a real application in the family.

But we expect even more of this derivation of the group from the primal horde. It ought also to help us to understand what is still incomprehensible and mysterious in group formations—all that lies hidden behind the enigmatic words hypnosis and suggestion. And I think it can succeed in this too. Let us recall that hypnosis has something positively uncanny about it; but the characteristic of uncanniness suggests something old and familiar that has undergone repression.[1] Let us consider how hypnosis is induced. The hypnotist asserts that he is in possession of a mysterious power which robs the subject of his own will, or, which is the same thing, the subject believes it of him. This mysterious power (which is even now

[1] 'Das Unheimliche.' *Imago*, 1919, Bd. V.

often described popularly as animal magnetism) must be the same that is looked upon by primitive people as the source of taboo, the same that emanates from kings and chieftains and makes it dangerous to approach them (*mana*). The hypnotist, then, is supposed to be in possession of this power; and how does he manifest it? By telling the subject to look him in the eyes; his most typical method of hypnotising is by his look. But it is precisely the sight of the chieftain that is dangerous and unbearable for primitive people, just as later that of the Godhead is for mortals. Even Moses had to act as an intermediary between his people and Jehovah, since the people could not support the sight of God; and when he returned from the presence of God his face shone— some of the *mana* had been transferred on to him, just as happens with the intermediary among primitive people.[1]

It is true that hypnosis can also be evoked in other ways, for instance by fixing the eyes upon a bright object or by listening to a monotonous sound. This is misleading and has given occasion to inadequate physiological theories. As a matter of fact these procedures merely serve to divert conscious attention and to hold it riveted. The situation is the same as if the hypnotist had said to the subject:

[1] See *Totem und Tabu* and the sources there quoted.

'Now concern yourself exclusively with my person; the rest of the world is quite uninteresting.' It would of course be technically inexpedient for a hypnotist to make such a speech; it would tear the subject away from his unconscious attitude and stimulate him to conscious opposition. The hypnotist avoids directing the subject's conscious thoughts towards his own intentions, and makes the person upon whom he is experimenting sink into an activity in which the world is bound to seem uninteresting to him; but at the same time the subject is in reality unconsciously concentrating his whole attention upon the hypnotist, and is getting into an attitude of *rapport*, of transference on to him. Thus the indirect methods of hypnotising, like many of the technical procedures used in making jokes, have the effect of checking certain distributions of mental energy which would interfere with the course of events in the unconscious, and they lead eventually to the same result as the direct methods of influence by means of staring or stroking.[1]

---

[1] This situation, in which the subject's attitude is unconsciously directed towards the hypnotist, while he is consciously occupied with monotonous and uninteresting perceptions, finds a parallel among the events of psycho-analytic treatment, which deserves to be mentioned here. At least once in the course of every analysis a moment comes when the patient obstinately maintains that just now positively nothing whatever occurs to his mind. His free associations come to a stop and the usual

Ferenczi has made the true discovery that when a hypnotist gives the command to sleep, which is often done at the beginning of hypnosis, he is putting himself in the place of the subject's parents. He thinks that two sorts of hypnosis are to be distinguished : one coaxing and soothing, which he considers is modelled upon the mother, and another threatening, which is derived from the father.[1] Now the command to sleep in hypnosis means nothing more nor less than an order to withdraw all interest from the world and to concentrate it upon the person of the hypnotist. And it is so understood by the subject; for in this withdrawal of interest from the outer world lies the psychological characteristic of sleep, and the kinship between sleep and the state of hypnosis is based upon it.

---

incentives for putting them in motion fail in their effect. As a result of pressure the patient is at last induced to admit that he is thinking of the view from the consulting-room window, of the wall-paper that he sees before him, or of the gas-lamp hanging from the ceiling. Then one knows at once that he has gone off into the transference and that he is engaged upon what are still unconscious thoughts relating to the physician; and one sees the stoppage in the patient's associations disappear, as soon as he has been given this explanation.

[1] Ferenczi: 'Introjektion und Übertragung.' *Jahrbuch der Psychoanalyse*, 1909, Bd. I. [*Contributions to Psycho-Analysis.* Boston, Badger, 1916, Chapter II.]

By the measures that he takes, then, the hypnotist awakens in the subject a portion of his archaic inheritance which had also made him compliant towards his parents and which had experienced an individual re-animation in his relation to his father; what is thus awakened is the idea of a paramount and dangerous personality, towards whom only a passive-masochistic attitude is possible, to whom one's will has to be surrendered,—while to be alone with him, 'to look him in the face', appears a hazardous enterprise. It is only in some such way as this that we can picture the relation of the individual member of the primal horde to the primal father. As we know from other reactions, individuals have preserved a variable degree of personal aptitude for reviving old situations of this kind. Some knowledge that in spite of everything hypnosis is only a game, a deceptive renewal of these old impressions, may however remain behind and take care that there is a resistance against any too serious consequences of the suspension of the will in hypnosis.

The uncanny and coercive characteristics of group formations, which are shown in their suggestion phenomena, may therefore with justice be traced back to the fact of their origin from the primal horde. The leader of the group is still the dreaded primal father; the group still wishes to be governed by unrestricted force; it has an extreme passion for authority; in Le Bon's phrase, it has a thirst for obedience. The primal father is the group ideal, which governs the ego in the place of the ego ideal. Hypnosis has a good claim to being described as a group of two; there remains as a definition for suggestion—a conviction which is not based upon perception and reasoning but upon an erotic tie.[1]

---

[1] It seems to me worth emphasizing the fact that the discussions in this section have induced us to give up Bernheim's conception of hypnosis and go back to the *naïf* earlier one. According to Bernheim all hypnotic phenomena are to be traced to the factor of suggestion, which is not itself capable of further explanation. We have come to the conclusion that suggestion is a partial manifestation of the state of hypnosis, and that hypnosis is solidly founded upon a predisposition which has survived in the unconscious from the early history of the human family.

XI

A DIFFERENTIATING GRADE IN THE EGO

If we survey the life of an individual man of to-day, bearing in mind the mutually complementary accounts of group psychology given by the authorities, we may lose the courage, in face of the complications that are revealed, to attempt a comprehensive exposition. Each individual is a component part of numerous groups, he is bound by ties of identification in many directions, and he has built up his ego ideal upon the most various models. Each individual therefore has a share in numerous group minds—those of his race, of his class, of his creed, of his nationality, etc.—and he can also raise himself above them to the extent of having a scrap of independence and originality. Such stable and lasting group formations, with their uniform and constant effects, are less striking to an observer than the rapidly formed and transient groups from which Le Bon has made his brilliant psychological character sketch of the group mind. And it is just in these noisy ephemeral groups, which are as it were superimposed upon the others, that we are met by the prodigy of the complete, even though only temporary, disappearance of exactly what we have recognized as individual acquirements.

We have interpreted this prodigy as meaning that the individual gives up his ego ideal and substitutes for it the group ideal as embodied in the leader. And we must add by way of correction that the prodigy is not equally great in every case. In many individuals the separation between the ego and the ego ideal is not very far advanced; the two still coincide readily; the ego has often preserved its earlier self-complacency. The selection of the leader is very much facilitated by this circumstance. He need only possess the typical qualities of the individuals concerned in a particularly clearly marked and pure form, and need only give an impression of greater force and of more freedom of libido; and in that case the need for a strong chief will often meet him half-way and invest him with a predominance to which he would otherwise perhaps have had no claim. The other members of the group, whose ego ideal would not, apart from this, have become embodied in his person without some correction, are then carried away with the rest by 'suggestion', that is to say, by means of identification.

We are aware that what we have been able to contribute towards the explanation of the libidinal structure of groups leads back to the distinction between the ego and the ego ideal and to the double kind of tie which this makes possible—identification, and substitution of the object for the ego ideal. The assumption of this kind of differentiating grade [*Stufe*] in the ego as a first step in an analysis of the ego must gradually establish its justification in the most various regions of psychology. In my paper 'Zur Einführung des Narzissmus' I have put together all the pathological material that could at the moment be used in support of this separation. But it may be expected that when we penetrate deeper into the psychology of the psychoses its significance will be discovered to be far greater. Let us reflect that the ego now appears in the relation of an object to the ego ideal which has been developed out of it, and that all the interplay between an outer object and the ego as a whole, with which our study of the neuroses has made us acquainted, may possibly be repeated upon this new scene of action inside the ego.

In this place I shall only follow up one of the consequences which seem possible from this point of view, thus resuming the discussion of a problem which I was obliged to leave unsolved elsewhere.[1] Each of the mental differentiations that we have become acquainted with represents a fresh aggravation of the difficulties of mental functioning, increases its

[1] 'Trauer und Melancholie.'

instability, and may become the starting-point for its breakdown, that is, for the onset of a disease. Thus, by being born we have made the step from an absolutely self-sufficient narcissism to the perception of a changing outer world and to the beginnings of the discovery of objects. And with this is associated the fact that we cannot endure the new state of things for long, that we periodically revert from it, in our sleep, to our former condition of absence of stimulation and avoidance of objects. It is true, however, that in this we are following a hint from the outer world, which, by means of the periodical change of day and night, temporarily withdraws the greater part of the stimuli that affect us. The second example, which is pathologically more important, is not subject to any such qualification. In the course of our development we have effected a separation of our mental existence into a coherent ego and into an unconscious and repressed portion which is left outside it; and we know that the stability of this new acquisition is exposed to constant shocks. In dreams and in neuroses what is thus excluded knocks for admission at the gates, guarded though they are by resistances; and in our waking health we make use of special artifices for allowing what is repressed to circumvent the resistances and for receiving it temporarily into our ego to the increase of our pleasure. Wit and humour, and to some extent the comic in general, may be regarded in this light. Everyone acquainted with the psychology of the neuroses will think of similar examples of less importance; but I hasten on to the application I have in view.

It is quite conceivable that the separation of the ego ideal from the ego cannot be borne for long either, and has to be temporarily undone. In all renunciations and limitations imposed upon the ego a periodical infringement of the prohibition is the rule; this indeed is shown by the institution of festivals, which in origin are nothing more nor less than excesses provided by law and which owe their cheerful character to the release which they bring.[1] The Saturnalia of the Romans and our modern carnival agree in this essential feature with the festivals of primitive people, which usually end in debaucheries of every kind and the transgression of what are at other times the most sacred commandments. But the ego ideal comprises the sum of all the limitations in which the ego has to acquiesce, and for that reason the abrogation of the ideal would necessarily be a magnificent festival for the ego, which might then once again feel satisfied with itself.[2]

[1] *Totem und Tabu.*

[2] Trotter traces repression back to the herd instinct. It is a translation of this into another form of expression rather than a contradiction when I say in my 'Einführung des Narzissmus' that on the part of the ego the construction of an ideal is the condition of repression.

H

always a feeling of triumph when
n the ego coincides with the ego ideal.
sense of guilt (as well as the sense of
ty) can also be understood as an expression
nsion between the ego and the ego ideal.

It is well known that there are people the general colour of whose mood oscillates periodically from an excessive depression through some kind of intermediate state to an exalted sense of well-being. These oscillations appear in very different degrees of amplitude, from what is just noticeable to those extreme instances which, in the shape of melancholia and mania, make the most painful or disturbing inroads upon the life of the person concerned. In typical cases of this cyclical depression outer exciting causes do not seem to play any decisive part; as regards inner motives, nothing more (or nothing different) is to be found in these patients than in all others. It has consequently become the custom to consider these cases as not being psychogenic. We shall refer later on to those other exactly similar cases of cyclical depression which can nevertheless easily be traced back to mental traumata.

Thus the foundation of these spontaneous oscillations of mood is unknown; we are without insight into the mechanism of the displacement of a melancholia by a mania. So we are free to suppose that these patients are people in whom our conjecture might find an actual application—their ego ideal might be temporarily resolved into their ego after having previously ruled it with especial strictness.

Let us keep to what is clear: On the basis of our analysis of the ego it cannot be doubted that in cases of mania the ego and the ego ideal have fused together, so that the person, in a mood of triumph and self-satisfaction, disturbed by no self-criticism, can enjoy the abolition of his inhibitions, his feelings of consideration for others, and his self-reproaches. It is not so obvious, but nevertheless very probable, that the misery of the melancholiac is the expression of a sharp conflict between the two faculties of his ego, — a conflict in which the ideal, in an excess of sensitiveness, relentlessly exhibits its condemnation of the ego in delusions of inferiority and in self-depreciation. The only question is whether we are to look for the causes of these altered relations between the ego and the ego ideal in the periodic rebellions, which we have postulated above, against the new institution, or whether we are to make other circumstances responsible for them.

A change into mania is not an indispensable feature of the symptomatology of melancholic depression. There are simple melancholias, some in single and some in recurring attacks, which never show this development. On the other hand there are melancholias in which the exciting cause clearly plays an aetiological part. They are those which occur after the loss of a loved object, whether by death or as a result of circumstances which have necessitated the withdrawal of the libido from the object. A psychogenic melancholia of this sort can end in mania, and this cycle can be repeated several times, just as easily as in a case which appears to be spontaneous. Thus the state of things is somewhat obscure, especially as only a few forms and cases of melancholia have been submitted to psycho-analytical investigation.[1] So far we only understand those cases in which the object is given up because it has shown itself unworthy of love. It is then set up again inside the ego, by means of identification, and severely condemned by the ego ideal. The reproaches and attacks directed towards the object come to light in the shape of melancholic self-reproaches.[2]

A melancholia of this kind may also end in a change to mania; so that the possibility of this happening represents a feature which is independent of the other characteristics in the symptomatology.

---

[1] Cf. Abraham: 'Ansätze zur psychoanalytischen Erforschung und Behandlung des manisch-depressiven Irreseins', 1912, in *Klinische Beiträge zur Psychoanalyse*, 1921.

[2] To speak more accurately, they conceal themselves behind the reproaches directed towards the person's own ego, and lend them the fixity, tenacity, and imperativeness which characterize the self-reproaches of a melancholiac.

Nevertheless I see no difficulty in assigning to the factor of the periodical rebellion of the ego against the ego ideal a share in both kinds of melancholia, the psychogenic as well as the spontaneous. In the spontaneous kind it may be supposed that the ego ideal is inclined to display a peculiar strictness, which then results automatically in its temporary suspension. In the psychogenic kind the ego would be incited to rebellion by ill-treatment on the part of its ideal—an ill-treatment which it encounters when there has been identification with a rejected object.

XII

POSTSCRIPT

In the course of the enquiry which has just been brought to a provisional end we came across a number of side-paths which we avoided pursuing in the first instance but in which there was much that offered us promises of insight. We propose now to take up a few of the points that have been left on one side in this way.

A. The distinction between identification of the ego with an object and replacement of the ego ideal by an object finds an interesting illustration in the two great artificial groups which we began by studying, the army and the Christian church.

It is obvious that a soldier takes his superior, that is, really, the leader of the army, as his ideal, while he identifies himself with his equals, and derives from this community of their egos the obligations for giving mutual help and for sharing possessions which comradeship implies. But he becomes ridiculous if he tries to identify himself with the general. The soldier in *Wallensteins Lager* laughs at the sergeant for this very reason:

> Wie er räuspert und wie er spuckt,
> Das habt ihr ihm glücklich abgeguckt ![1]

It is otherwise in the Catholic Church. Every Christian loves Christ as his ideal and feels himself united with all other Christians by the tie of identification. But the Church requires more of him. He has also to identify himself with Christ and love all other Christians as Christ loved them. At both points, therefore, the Church requires that the position of the libido which is given by a group formation should be supplemented. Identification has to be added where object-choice has taken place, and object love where there is identification. This addition evidently goes beyond the constitution of the group. One can be a good Christian and yet be far from the idea of putting oneself in Christ's place and of having like him an all-embracing love for mankind. One need not think oneself capable, weak mortal that one is, of the Saviour's largeness of soul and strength of love. But this further development in the distribution of libido in the group is probably the factor upon which Christianity bases its claim to have reached a higher ethical level.

[1] [Literally: 'How he clears his throat and how he spits, that you have cleverly copied from him.']

B. We have said that it would be possible to specify the point in the mental development of man at which the advance from group to individual psychology was also achieved by the individual members of the group.[1]

For this purpose we must return for a moment to the scientific myth of the father of the primal horde. He was later on exalted into the creator of the world, and with justice, for he had produced all the sons who composed the first group. He was the ideal of each one of them, at once feared and honoured, a fact which led later to the idea of taboo. These many individuals eventually banded themselves together, killed him and cut him in pieces. None of the group of victors could take his place, or, if one of them did, the battles began afresh, until they understood that they must all renounce their father's heritage. They then formed the totemistic community of brothers, all with equal rights and united by the totem prohibitions which were to preserve and to expiate the memory of the murder. But the dissatisfaction with what had been achieved still remained, and it became the source of new developments. The persons who were united in this group of brothers gradually came towards a revival

---

[1] What follows at this point was written under the influence of an exchange of ideas with Otto Rank.

of the old state of things at a new level. Man became once more the chief of a family, and broke down the prerogatives of the gynaecocracy which had become established during the fatherless period. As a compensation for this he may at that time have acknowledged the mother deities, whose priests were castrated for the mother's protection, after the example that had been given by the father of the primal horde. And yet the new family was only a shadow of the old one; there were numbers of fathers and each one was limited by the rights of the others.

It was then, perhaps, that some individual, in the exigency of his longing, may have been moved to free himself from the group and take over the father's part. He who did this was the first epic poet; and the advance was achieved in his imagination. This poet disguised the truth with lies in accordance with his longing. He invented the heroic myth. The hero was a man who by himself had slain the father —the father who still appeared in the myth as a totemistic monster. Just as the father had been the boy's first ideal, so in the hero who aspires to the father's place the poet now created the first ego ideal. The transition to the hero was probably afforded by the youngest son, the mother's favourite, whom she had protected from paternal jealousy, and who, in the era of the primal horde, had been the father's successor. In the lying poetic fancies of prehistoric times the woman, who had been the prize of battle and the allurement to murder, was probably turned into the seducer and instigator to the crime.

The hero claims to have acted alone in accomplishing the deed, which certainly only the horde as a whole would have ventured upon. But, as Rank has observed, fairy tales have preserved clear traces of the facts which were disavowed. For we often find in them that the hero who has to carry out some difficult task (usually a youngest son, and not infrequently one who has represented himself to the father surrogate as being stupid, that is to say, harmless)—we often find, then, that this hero can carry out his task only by the help of a crowd of small animals, such as bees or ants. These would be the brothers in the primal horde, just as in the same way in dream symbolism insects or vermin signify brothers and sisters (contemptuously, considered as babies). Moreover every one of the tasks in myths and fairy tales is easily recognisable as a substitute for the heroic deed.

The myth, then, is the step by which the individual emerges from group psychology. The first myth was certainly the psychological, the hero myth; the explanatory nature myth must have followed much later. The poet who had taken this step and had in this way set himself free from the group in his imagination, is nevertheless able (as Rank has further observed) to find his way back to it in reality. For he goes and relates to the group his hero's deeds which he has invented. At bottom this hero is no one but himself. Thus he lowers himself to the level of reality, and raises his hearers to the level of imagination. But his hearers understand the poet, and, in virtue of their having the same relation of longing towards the primal father, they can identify themselves with the hero.[1]

The lie of the heroic myth culminates in the deification of the hero. Perhaps the deified hero may have been earlier than the Father God and may have been a precursor to the return of the primal father as a deity. The series of gods, then, would run chronologically: Mother Goddess—Hero— Father God. But it is only with the elevation of the never forgotten primal father that the deity acquires the features that we still recognise in him to-day.[2]

C. A great deal has been said in this paper about directly sexual instincts and those that are inhibited

[1] Cf. Hanns Sachs: 'Gemeinsame Tagträume', a summary made by the lecturer himself of a paper read at the Sixth Psycho-analytical Congress, held at the Hague in 1920. *Internationale Zeitschrift für Psychoanalyse*, 1920, Bd. VI. ['Day-Dreams in Common'. *International Journal of Psycho-Analysis*, 1920, Vol. I.]

[2] In this brief exposition I have made no attempt to bring forward any of the material existing in legends, myths, fairy tales, the history of manners, etc., in support of the construction.

in their aims, and it may be hoped that this distinction will not meet with too much resistance. But a detailed discussion of the question will not be out of place, even if it only repeats what has to a great extent already been said before.

The development of the libido in children has made us acquainted with the first but also the best example of sexual instincts which are inhibited in their aims. All the feelings which a child has towards its parents and those who look after it pass by an easy transition into the wishes which give expression to the child's sexual tendencies. The child claims from these objects of its love all the signs of affection which it knows of; it wants to kiss them, touch them, and look at them; it is curious to see their genitals, and to be with them when they perform their intimate excremental functions; it promises to marry its mother or nurse—whatever it ·may understand by that; it proposes to itself to bear its father a child, etc. Direct observation, as well as the subsequent analytic investigation of the residue of childhood, leave no doubt as to the complete fusion of tender and jealous feelings and of sexual intentions, and show us in what a fundamental way the child makes the person it loves into the object of all its incompletely centred sexual tendencies.[1]

[1] Cf. *Drei Abhandlungen zur Sexualtheorie.*

This first configuration of the child's love, which in typical cases is co-ordinated with the Oedipus complex, succumbs, as we know, from the beginning of the period of latency onwards to a wave of repression. Such of it as is left over shows itself as a purely tender emotional tie, which relates to the same people, but is no longer to be described as 'sexual'. Psychoanalysis, which illuminates the depths of mental life, has no difficulty in showing that the sexual ties of the earliest years of childhood also persist, though repressed and unconscious. It gives us courage to assert that wherever we come across a tender feeling it is the successor to a completely 'sensual' object tie with the person in question or rather with that person's prototype (or *imago*). It cannot indeed disclose to us without a special investigation whether in a given case this former complete sexual current still exists under repression or whether it has already been exhausted. To put it still more precisely: it is quite certain that it is still there as a form and possibility, and can always be charged with cathectic energy and put into activity again by means of regression; the only question is (and it cannot always be answered) what degree of cathexis and operative force it still has at the present moment. Equal care must be taken in this connection to avoid two sources of error—the Scylla of under-estimating the importance of the repressed unconscious, and the Charybdis of judging the normal entirely by the standards of the pathological.

A psychology which will not or cannot penetrate the depths of what is repressed regards tender emotional ties as being invariably the expression of tendencies which have no sexual aim, even though they are derived from tendencies which have such an aim.[1]

We are justified in saying that they have been diverted from these sexual aims, even though there is some difficulty in giving a representation of such a diversion of aim which will conform to the requirements of metapsychology. Moreover, those instincts which are inhibited in their aims always preserve some few of their original sexual aims; even an affectionate devotee, even a friend or an admirer, desires the physical proximity and the sight of the person who is now loved only in the 'Pauline' sense. If we choose, we may recognise in this diversion of aim a beginning of the *sublimation* of the sexual instincts, or on the other hand we may fix the limits of sublimation at some more distant point. Those sexual instincts which are inhibited in their aims have a great functional advantage over those which are uninhibited. Since they are not capable of really

[1] Hostile feelings, which are a little more complicated in their construction, offer no exception to this rule.

complete satisfaction, they are especially adapted to create permanent ties; while those instincts which are directly sexual incur a loss of energy each time they are satisfied, and must wait to be renewed by a fresh accumulation of sexual libido, so that meanwhile the object may have been changed. The inhibited instincts are capable of any degree of admixture with the uninhibited; they can be transformed back into them, just as they arose out of them. It is well known how easily erotic wishes develop out of emotional relations of a friendly character, based upon appreciation and admiration, (compare Molière's 'Embrassez-moi pour l'amour du grec'), between a master and a pupil, between a performer and a delighted listener, and especially in the case of women. In fact the growth of emotional ties of this kind, with their purposeless beginnings, provides a much frequented pathway to sexual object-choice. Pfister, in his *Frömmigkeit des Grafen von Zinzendorf,*[1] has given an extremely clear and certainly not an isolated example of how easily even an intense religious tie can revert to ardent sexual excitement. On the other hand it is also very usual for directly sexual tendencies, short-lived in themselves, to be transformed into a lasting and purely tender tie;

---

[1] [*Schriften zur angewandten Seelenkunde.* Heft 8. Vienna, Deuticke, 1910.]

and the consolidation of a passionate love marriage rests to a large extent upon this process.

We shall naturally not be surprised to hear that the sexual tendencies that are inhibited in their aims arise out of the directly sexual ones when inner or outer obstacles make the sexual aims unattainable. The repression during the period of latency is an inner obstacle of this kind—or rather one which has become inner. We have assumed that the father of the primal horde owing to his sexual intolerance compelled all his sons to be abstinent, and thus forced them into ties that were inhibited in their aims, while he reserved for himself freedom of sexual enjoyment and in this way remained without ties. All the ties upon which a group depends are of the character of instincts that are inhibited in their aims. But here we have approached the discussion of a new subject, which deals with the relation between directly sexual instincts and the formation of groups.

D. The last two remarks will have prepared us for finding that directly sexual tendencies are unfavourable to the formation of groups. In the history of the development of the family there have also, it is true, been group relations of sexual love (group marriages); but the more important sexual love became for the ego, and the more it developed the characteristics of being in love, the more urgently it required to be limited to two people—*una cum uno*—as is prescribed by the nature of the genital aim. Polygamous inclinations had to be content to find satisfaction in a succession of changing objects.

Two people coming together for the purpose of sexual satisfaction, in so far as they seek for solitude, are making a demonstration against the herd instinct, the group feeling. The more they are in love, the more completely they suffice for each other. The rejection of the group's influence is manifested in the shape of a sense of shame. The extremely violent feelings of jealousy are summoned up in order to protect the sexual object-choice from being encroached upon by a group tie. It is only when the tender, that is, the personal, factor of a love relation gives place entirely to the sensual one, that it is possible for two people to have sexual intercourse in the presence of others or for there to be simultaneous sexual acts in a group as occurs at an orgy. But at that point a regression has taken place to an early stage in sexual relations, at which being in love as yet played no part, and all sexual objects were judged to be of equal value, somewhat in the sense of Bernard Shaw's malicious aphorism to the effect that being in love means greatly exaggerating the difference between one woman and another.

There are abundant indications that being in love only made its appearance late on in the sexual relations between men and women; so that the

I

opposition between sexual love and group ties is also a late development. Now it may seem as though this assumption were incompatible with our myth of the primal family. For it was after all by their love for their mothers and sisters that the troop of brothers was, as we have supposed, driven to parricide; and it is difficult to imagine this love as being anything but unbroken and primitive—that is. as an intimate union of the tender and the sensual. But further consideration resolves this objection into a confirmation. One of the reactions to the parricide was after all the institution of totemistic exogamy, the prohibition of any sexual relation with those women of the family who had been tenderly loved since childhood. In this way a wedge was driven in between a man's tender and sensual feelings, one still firmly fixed in his erotic life to-day.[1] As a result of this exogamy the sensual needs of men had to be satisfied with strange and unloved women.

In the great artificial groups, the church and the army, there is no room for woman as a sexual object. The love relation between men and women remains outside these organisations. Even where groups are formed which are composed of both men and women the distinction between the sexes plays no part. There is scarcely any sense in asking whether

---

[1] See 'Über die allgemeinste Erniedrigung des Liebeslebens.'

the libido which keeps groups together is of a homosexual or of a heterosexual nature, for it is not
differentiated according to the sexes, and particularly
shows a complete disregard for the aims of the genital
organisation of the libido.

Even in a person who has in other respects become
absorbed in a group the directly sexual tendencies
preserve a little of his individual activity. If they
become too strong they disintegrate every group
formation. The Catholic Church had the best of
motives for recommending its followers to remain
unmarried and for imposing celibacy upon its priests;
but falling in love has often driven even priests to
leave the church. In the same way love for women
breaks through the group ties of race, of national
separation, and of the social class system, and it
thus produces important effects as a factor in civili-
zation. It seems certain that homosexual love is
far more compatible with group ties, even when it
takes the shape of uninhibited sexual tendencies—a
remarkable fact, the explanation of which might carry
us far.

The psycho-analytic investigation of the psycho-
neuroses has taught us that their symptoms are to
be traced back to directly sexual tendencies which
are repressed but still remain active. We can complete
this formula by adding to it: or, to tendencies inhibited
in their aims, whose inhibition has not been entirely

successful or has made room for a return to the repressed sexual aim. It is in accordance with this that a neurosis should make its victim asocial and should remove him from the usual group formations. It may be said that a neurosis has the same disintegrating effect upon a group as being in love. On the other hand it appears that where a powerful impetus has been given to group formation neuroses may diminish and at all events temporarily disappear. Justifiable attempts have also been made to turn this antagonism between neuroses and group formation to therapeutic account. Even those who do not regret the disappearance of religious illusions from the civilized world of to-day will admit that so long as they were in force they offered those who were bound by them the most powerful protection against the danger of neurosis. Nor is it hard to discern in all the ties with mystico-religious or philosophico-religious sects and communities the manifestation of distorted cures of all kinds of neuroses. All of this is bound up with the contrast between directly sexual tendencies and those which are inhibited in their aims.

If he is left to himself, a neurotic is obliged to replace by his own symptom formations the great group formations from which he is excluded. He creates his own world of imagination for himself, his own religion, his own system of delusions, and thus

is extraordinarily rich in content, for it embraces all possible relations between the ego and the object—both those in which the object is retained and others in which it is abandoned or erected inside the ego itself—and also the conflicting relations between the ego and its ego ideal.

INDEX

MADE AND PRINTED IN GREAT BRITAIN BY
LOWE AND BRYDONE PRINTERS LIMITED, LONDON, N.W.10